Programmed Perceptions

Programmed Perceptions

TaNeisha R. Page PhD

ISBN-13: 9781535049320
ISBN-10: 1535049324
Library of Congress Control Number: 2016911160
CreateSpace Independent Publishing Platform
North Charleston, South Carolina

Table of Contents

Dedication

This book is dedicated to my younger sister Trenati. Her generation is the future of this Country and it is imperative they all educate themselves on this topic.

Preface

In America so many different groups of people are trying to break the mold and change their life trajectory. African Americans are in a spot where we find ourselves vulnerable to different situations that happen every day. Since black people were slaves we have been seen as *second-class citizens in American society*. From the way we are portrayed in the media, how the criminal justice system works against us, and how black people are held to a higher standard than other races yet still treated as though we are less than. There is a disillusion that since we have a black President of the United States, that the mistreatment of black people has stopped. The reality is, having a black President might have proven how strong and resilient black people can be, which in turn created more of a fear that black people are just as capable as anyone else.

For centuries black people have had to prove their worth and find ways to overcome the skepticism we are often faced with. This book is not only an informative outlook of what African American's experience in their lives but, even more so, a book that will create more self-reflections within ourselves in hopes of being part of the solution rather than part of the problem. It is my hope this awareness can create a thought provoking discourse that will help us, as a society, move toward being more accepting, understanding, and supportive. Unfortunately, we are becoming desensitized over the unfair events that happen to black people on a daily basis and this is something that needs to be addressed. Exclusion for some and liberty for others is not what this Country is built on.

It is no longer acceptable to not be aware of the inequities that happen every day. It doesn't matter your race, ethnicity, religion, sexual preference, gender identity or sex identity, every single one of us needs to be a part of cultivating sustainable and effective change! Every single person that might have been a victim of discrimination, been a supporter of discrimination or would like to act like discrimination doesn't exist! We are all in this together and together is the only way we can progress in a positive, honest, consistent, racial blind, reflective society.

This book will cause some discomfort, confusion, and maybe even anger. However, the truth is these are standard emotions that should be experienced when discussing inequities of people.

"Education brings self-respect."

~ Muhammad Ali

One

I Pledge

Introduction

One of the hardest jobs in America is being black. The reason is because we live in a society where black people are seen as criminals or liabilities more than they are seen as normal functional members of society. We constantly fight perceptions that get placed on us, as well as battling our own doubts and fears. Yes, we have a black president, but that does not mean the entire country has started to accept black people as capable individuals. Now, more than ever, the injustices, prejudices, and blatant discriminations are identified more readily and openly—thanks to social media. Real-time communication has given us the ability to know what the media is actually reporting, has opened discussions surrounding real issues, and made it possible to record events as they happen in our communities. The truth is black parents have to have different types of conversations with their children than parents of other races. Those conversations include how society sees black people as threats, understanding confrontational situations to avoid, learning how to not act "too black," and avoiding drawing unwanted attention to ourselves. No longer is it safe to be black and live in a great community;

it is making sure that people—in particular, people in power—are not threatened by our mere existence.

I refer to black people as "us" and "we" in this book, as a way to redefine how I see black people as a group that I not only identify with—but, also as a way for me to pull away from the traditional sense of "them" and "they," as "we" are commonly referred to by society's standards. Additionally, it will help readers understand the very meaning of "othering," as people tend to "other" black people through racism and discrimination, whether intentional or unintentional. In many ways, I feel compelled to commit to a unified term that is so much more than a label for black people. It is a way to see us as individuals who garner strength and unity through words that often separate us, discriminate us, and are used against us. Therefore, black people as "us" and "we" are grounded in meaning that is deeper than a label. It is a way to understand that I stand by how I tell my story, and more importantly, it is how I share my experiences with the experiences of black people as a whole because of our skin color.

Just as people find themselves referring to others via terms that identify them by color, some people do not realize they are racist nor have racist thoughts because they are embedded within them. Often, this is through what they have seen in their own experiences, the way they were raised, or the ways they have understood their own ideas of how black people are in general. However, these thoughts and opinions can change if people are given the right information and understand that black people are just like any other race. We have challenges and successes just like any other race. Internally, as black people, we are programmed to be on alert. When a cop pulls up behind us on the highway our initial reaction is usually to make sure we are following all the traffic laws. When we do not get a job we feel we are qualified for, when we feel like we are getting treated differently, and we feel that we are not receiving the same opportunities as others, it is just another way to apply race to our everyday lives. At some point in the situation, we wonder if our race played a role in the outcome of a situation.

2

Black communities are not given the opportunities, resources, respect, or power that most other communities are given. If you don't believe me, I want to challenge you to go drive around a black community. Count how many educational signs, Chick-Fil-A's, Starbucks, political signs, or signs of positivity you see as you pass by. On the opposite end of that, count how many cop cars, policeman bail bonds signs, murals, loans, and advertisements for unhealthy foods you see. If you listen to the news or what police officers say, they will tell you that more crime is happening in black communities versus other communities. However, the truth is crime is happening everywhere and the people who will be caught doing the crime are those operating where the authorities are located to catch them. Let's be honest, how can someone get arrested or get in trouble when the cops aren't around?

When you are part of the dominant, white culture you never have to stop and think about how your behaviors reflect on you because everything that you do is considered the social standard. In 2008, when Barack Obama won the presidential race, it was a time where I became more aware of the fact that I was black. It sounds silly because I am black every day, but during that time, I felt constantly under attack. Why? On social media accounts, I began to notice tons of personal attacks on black people. This was not because people didn't think Barack Obama was qualified to do the job, but because he was a black man now representing an entire country. People who were "friends," bosses, and former co-workers were all commenting on President Obama's race almost like that immediately meant he would be a terrible president. The color of his skin dictated people's behaviors and comments. The man had not even been sworn into office, but he was being crucified. People can say this didn't have anything to do with race, but what else were they judging him on?

Unfortunately, this is something that happens often. Recently, Beyoncé released a song titled "Formation." This video brought to light what being black in America looks like. Just to name a few things, there was a black child walking around with his hands up in protest, Beyoncé being proud of "things that make her black," and Beyoncé seeming to drown at the end of the music video on a cop car in what looked like a resemblance of Hurricane Katrina. She went on to perform a little bit of her song at Super Bowl 50. Not 30 minutes after she was finished with her performance, people on social media started to talk about how Beyoncé was knocking cops. Now let's think about this for a second. How in the world is Beyoncé knocking on cops? She created a song and a video about her life experience, from her perspective. Nothing different than any other artist who creates music. But yet, she gets branded with hating cops? I see two things about this that make it interesting. First, Beyoncé has many fans across the world. People in America love her and see her as an inspiration. THAT is the threat! Beyoncé was bringing more attention to what is happening in these lower income communities that people do not often see, and that was seen as a threat to cops. That music video was not created based on things that she made up in her head; it was created based on events that have actually happened. There are events that made the world take a second look at how cops were treating black people. Secondly, if the cops were doing the things they needed to do, there would not be any controversy. What is wrong with her making an artistic video based on her perception of what she sees? That is the point of being an artist, which you can speak about what you want and you can put a music video out about whatever you want. It was interesting how the cops were not threatened when rappers spoke about killing, robbing (since these are direct crimes that cops will have to deal with head on), or anything else they want to talk about. But Beyoncé making a representation of what she sees is considered threatening. It is music; it is a way of self-expression. How is this a problem? The message gets missed because it is easier to discredit Beyoncé, rather than being able to hear the message, acknowledge it, and make some changes in our own daily lives.

When black people do something that is good, or represents their experiences, it is met with criticism. Imagine if President Obama was as aggressive, stern, and combative as Donald Trump? What if he would have talked about his penis size on a nationally televised debate? What if Michelle Obama had pictures like Melania Trump out there? Would the

Obamas get a free pass on these things? Would the press open up shows with quotes of President Obama being that dismissive and disrespectful to entire groups of people?

Now, consider the things within the black culture that have been around for years, but suddenly when someone outside of being black represents parts of it, they are inventing something new? To comment on other social examples, when Kim Kardashian started wearing her hair in braids after she gave birth to her second child, fashion blogs and the media were all excited about the "new style" she was bringing to the table. The truth behind the braids is that slaves wore their hair in braids many years ago. Kim Kardashian did not invent the style, but yet, she gets the credit for doing so. Now think about the term "southern food." Southern food is in essence soul food—which is food that black people have been making for years. Next, Miley Cyrus posted videos of her twerking and then twerking became a "thing." Black people have been twerking before Miley Cyrus, yet the credit goes to her. How is that when Miley Cyrus does it, it is a new fad? Why are black people not getting credit for these things? For years we have been fighting to be free and to be recognized for the things we bring to the table. We are past being defeated and feeling disappointed. For these reasons, change has to start happening soon. But in order for change to happen, we have to address the situations and environments that still prevent black people from being seen as equal people.

The rest of this section will highlight terminology and events that black people often have to deal with. These terms will be spread out throughout the book and are common themes that play a role in how black people are treated. Each term is interweaved into why we are treated the way we are, and how each of these terms rear their ugly heads and impact black people every day.

White Privilege

When the term White Privilege gets brought up, it creates different types of conversations and emotions. Some people see it is as an attack on white people, and other people instantly know what the term refers to. Let me be clear, this section on White Privilege is NOT an attack on white people. It is a way to show how society benefits white people and their experiences. In many ways, this section is to highlight the fact that white people don't have to endure the same experiences as black people because of these privileges.

A lot of time I see white privilege being talked about on social media accounts, and I can always count on a white person to reply with: "What am I supposed to do? Apologize for being white?" The answer is No. We were all born a certain color and there is no need to apologize for that. However, this is more about white people acknowledging or being aware of the fact that being white comes with certain privileges that are unseen. What am I referring to? There is a saying called, "Driving While Black." This is an example of white privilege. Black people are pulled over just because of their skin while white people do not have to worry about it. This is a privilege that is unseen. White people are not even aware that they do not have to be concerned about driving while white. Look at Trayvon Martin; he was walking home in a white neighborhood, and he was profiled even though he LIVED there for crying out loud. But because he was black, one man decided he did not belong in that neighborhood and took action. Another common white privilege is being well-spoken and educated because it is an expectation of being white. For example, when a black person speaks proper English and/or is educated, it is considered an accomplishment for that black person because white people are all expected to be well-spoken and educated. Another component of white privilege to take into consideration is that complimentary shampoos and conditioners are readily available in hotels. As another example of an unseen privileged experience, white people do not question whether the available shampoo and conditioner are there for them to use. If anything, the fact that these items are readily available for white people and not black people shows that the underlying privilege is that being white provides conveniences and expectations. If you have at least one black friend, perhaps you are aware that black people have to use different types of shampoos and conditioners than whites. Maybe this idea of privilege is a bit more obvious, now. In hotels there are always shampoos and conditioners in the restrooms that can be used in hotels. It is the same with the grocery stores. The white people shampoos and conditioners are in the hair product aisle. As for black people, our products tend to be in the "ethnic aisle." Even hair commercials are geared towards white people, unless you are watching a network with black shows. The fact is, black people do not have the luxury of having shampoo and conditioner available in hotels and grocery stores. Even when it comes to commercials, black hair products are not advertised. It is not a secret that black and white people have different hair textures, and because of that, black people need different types of shampoo and conditioner. White privilege allows for shampoo and conditioner to be readily available and accessible.

The reason why white privilege is hard for white people to grasp is because they do not have every day instances in life where they are treated differently because of the color of their skin. I once told a friend about my experience shopping in the middle of the day. I walked in to an expensive store in my workout clothes, in the middle of the day, with my hair up in a ponytail. During that time, I was followed around that store. I was constantly asked if I needed any help, or if I was finding everything okay. Behind me walked in an older white lady who was dressed similar to me. She got greeted and then she was left alone until she needed help. Now, I do not think for one second that lady knew that she was being treated differently than me. However, she was, and the only difference between the two of us was our race. For the record, at the time I was on a lunch break from a company where I was allowed to wear whatever I wanted to for work. The perception was probably that I did not have job, and that I could not afford anything in that store. Therefore, due to my skin color and these perceptions, I was treated differently.

Being white comes with privileges and these privileges make life easier. Whether you want the privileges or not, it does not matter because it is something that comes with being white. There are several times I have had to "check my blackness" before dealing with a situation. There is nothing wrong with a white person "checking their whiteness" just the same. Throughout this book, there will be more references to white privilege because it is my belief that this is a reason for a lot of the discrimination against blacks.

Token Black Person

As black people we immediately know what this phrase means. Unfortunately, any black person that has had a friend who is not familiar with black people has experienced being the token black person. This phrase can mean two things:

1. A black person who speaks for their entire race.
2. The one black person within a group that is successful or because they are "different" than other blacks.

Having a black person speak for an entire race happens to us in all environments, and this is something that does not happen to whites because every black person is a token at work, school and socially. This is like asking the one black person in their group to make sense of other black people. This usually starts with this common question: "Why do black people......?" Real-life examples of questions I have personally been asked include:

1. "TaNeisha, why don't you want to get your hair wet?"
2. "Why do black people talk so loud?"
3. "Do you smoke weed?"
4. "How come all black people can dance?"

These are just a few questions that have been asked of me that put me in a situation where I am answering for my entire race. Everyone has their individual way of doing things, and black people are no different. Just like other races, it depends on how you were raised, and what you are accustomed to. It is not simply because you are black that things are the way they are. Often times the "Token Black Person" will speak on behalf of all black people, and the reality is that one person cannot speak about any one particular race!

The second meaning of this phrase refers to the "good black person." This is the person who is in a circle, and is perceived as not having the same thoughts as black people not in the circle. Comments in this group include:

1. "You are not like other black people"
2. "Why don't you think like other black people?"

What this circle might not realize is that this person does have thoughts like "other black people" and they are "like other black people." But because of the setting they are in, they know if they were to act on it or even speak on it that would create conflict. Or even worse, it would have people looking at that black person differently in an already alienating environment. Imagine what it feels like to be the one black person amongst a group of 5 or 10 people? Anything you say can run the risk of being scrutinized or looked at differently. Even more annoying is then being asked questions that take us back to the first part of being the "token black person." It is a no-win situation.

The reason why being a token black person is being brought up here is because it needs to be brought into the conversation and acknowledged. This is part of the experience of black people, and it has become such a common occurrence that people do not even notice when they are doing it. It is important for black people to understand these situations—when they are in them—just as important as it is for people of other races to be careful of how you are asking questions. As a black person, you should never have to defend your race or try to find ways to make your race seem "normal" to a group of curious people.

Slavery

News flash; SLAVERY did happen. I want to repeat that there were slaves in America! Black people were seen as $^3/_5$ of a person during the time of slavery. It was important for slave owners to make their slaves completely dependent on them so they could continue to control their every move. They were restricted from learning how to read and write, and every single movement was monitored if it did not benefit their slave owners. Many slave owners took this control even further and sexually abused woman. Many times, the abuse occurred in front of their men. There was a divide and conquer plan by rewarding slaves who obeyed their masters with special privileges. Slaves who did not obey the rules were tortured and beaten as a consequence. This played a big role in keeping slaves divided and not allowing them to unify together. Keep in mind that these are people being told what to do by other people; their lives were not their own. They did not have a voice, and in fact, when slaves did try to speak up they were either brutally dealt with or sold. Often times, many of the slaves were taken away from their families.

Why is this important? Let's take a look at slavery back then and compare it to what is happening in 2016.

1. Being dependent on slave owners –
   In today's society, many black people are not given the same opportunities as whites. People making these decisions on who gets to do all of these things are white people. Looking at this from a slave perspective, black people still have "slave owners." We just call them directors, managers, principals, coaches, producers, CEO's, etc. Because they are the ones that get to make the decisions, it critically impacts how far a person can go in certain situations.
2. Restricted opportunities to learn how to read and write –
   Of course, at the first site of this it sounds ludicrous to think that black people are being restricted when it comes to learning to read and write. Let's take a closer look at this. Education starts in childhood, and most importantly, in Kindergarten. If a child is in a school system where they are not learning, or being exposed to, similar things found in a "higher end" school, they

are at a disadvantage. What about when you have kids who are in lower income neighborhoods, which means they go to lower income schools. Are we really going to fool ourselves into thinking a kid in a lower income school versus a privileged school is learning the same thing? What about when they go to middle school and high school? A student's performance and knowledge determine where they will go to college. Secondly, to get into a "better university" a student needs to be as smart and be just as educated as the other kids who are trying to go to that university. However, when you start off behind, how do you ever get caught up? Believe it or not, black children are restricted on how much they learn about reading and writing. Other facets of education leave them at a disadvantage. But, having a sizeable percentage of the student population entering the institution with a disadvantage helps universities bring in additional money because these students will have to take developmental courses.

3. Having movements monitored –
   Black people are profiled every single day, whether it is entering a grocery store, driving a car, clothes shopping, protesting, attending sporting events, or being in an airport. Anywhere that you can think of, black people are monitored and their behaviors are watched as well. At any point, the wrong movement can result in someone/authorities feeling threatened. This can result in the police being called, or if it is the police using violence that can lead to bodily harm; or even death. THIS HAPPENS ALL THE TIME!

4. Slaves being abused –
   Police brutality.

Considering all the elements that reflect similarities in slavery and what can be referred to as modern day slavery, is 2016 better than how it was in 1700's? Let's not forgot all the ways that black people are still looked at as less than. Black people have always been and still are oppressed, beaten, raped, stripped of their dignity, and looked at as servants every single day. This is a real struggle that is happening. Unless you have these types of experiences, you might not understand it. BUT the worst thing you can do is act like it did not, and does not still, happen. The propaganda you see in the media about black people will lead you to believe that we are aggressive, disrespectful, and ignorant. The truth is ALL HUMANS have the capability of being these things, not just blacks.

Understanding this Book

I know some people will not understand the things in this book, and some people might even view is as complaining. But I want to encourage you to seek out someone that you might know of color, and ask them about their life experiences. Tell them you are reading this book, and you want to know if anything in it is true. Some people live in such a way that they encounter the things in this book every day.

Open your eyes and do not be afraid of what you will find. Realizing and acknowledging the hardships that black people face does not mean that everything you know to be true is not true. It means there is still space to grow and do better for each other. We are all on Earth to make it a better place, but the only way we can do this is by listening, learning, and making a difference. Black people do not want pity, and we do not even want anyone to feel sorry for us and our struggles. But what we would love is to be treated as equal. Not just equal by saying we are equal and giving us have the same rights as others, but by showing that through action, we are equally respected for being people.

I use the term black throughout this book because that is how I self-identify. For me, black is inclusive of African Americans, colored people, or whatever other term that African Americans are usually called. This book is not an attack on other races, but more about giving imperative information to people of all races to understand what black people endure. After reading through this book, you might not fully understand the emotions that black people have or where the frustrations come from. However, you should have more insight into where those emotions come from and how they can impact someone's life. People are powerful. We all have the opportunity to cause major change and disrupt how things function. As you read the list of words below, I want you to close your eyes and think about what type of person comes to mind:

1. Rich
2. Aggressive
3. Happy
4. Black Man
5. Police Officer
6. Lawyer
7. Teacher
8. Athlete
9. Loud
10. Smart

Reflect on which words caused you to envision a black person and which words made you think of other races. Remember these answers as you read through the book and see how your own thoughts and experiences compare to those that are discussed.

"Racism is still with us. But it is up to us to prepare our children for what they have to meet, and, hopefully, we shall overcome."

~ Rosa Parks

TWO

MEDIA

...allegiance

The media has become a place where people believe they get all the facts about a story or situation. However, the sad thing about the media is that they have an agenda, which is driven by profit. Their goal is to increase their market share, which in turn boosts ratings, resulting in higher rates for advertising and/or subscriptions, generating higher profit margins. Having said that, these news outlets also have to carefully select which stories they cover, and most importantly, determine how to slant the stories to appeal to their viewers. For example, when Mike Brown, the unarmed black teen who was gunned down and killed in Missouri, the media had to make several decisions. Every channel took a different approach.

On one end of the spectrum, once news got out via tweets, Facebook posts, and YouTube videos that the cops were aggressively challenging protesters, CNN and MSNBC decided to broadcast live events, focusing on the frustrations of the communities to foster understanding and compassion. They began telling stories about the struggles that the community had endured over the past several years. The attention quickly shifted to peaceful protesters and stories their communities which helped viewers understand why the individuals living there were upset.

By day 3, statistics were reported that increased overall awareness of the grim, unrelenting oppression blacks face on a daily basis.

On the other end of the spectrum, FOX news focused only on the looters, choosing not to show the black people who were peacefully demonstrating. Additionally, the cops were shown suited up like military personnel. Each station had a panel of "experts" (and I use that word lightly because I do not think these people are experts; they were people who can tell a story and have a perspective that people either agree with or not) who debated different issues. Of course CNN and MSNBC focused on the neighborhoods and how cops had been treating people in their community. FOX, however, began blasting black people for not listening to the cops, citing reasons to place blame for the controversy squarely with the community. Here is the bigger issue at hand. On several occasions, after a basketball or football team wins a championship, there is looting; cars are turned over, fires are set, and other forms of chaos ensue. Why are these outbursts not televised just the same? Where is all the attention for these groups of people breaking the rules? There is one major difference between these two scenarios: in one case the participants are mostly black, while in the other they are mostly white.

Media in Sports

As an avid sports watcher, it is all too obvious how different athletes are treated in the media. Race is entrenched in sports media. It is present in the questions that are asked, the news that breaks, and how these individuals carry themselves professionally. Reporting on the sports does not mean that color boundaries do not exist. In the NFL, if Tom Brady is on the sideline yelling at his team trying to get his team together and get them fired up, he is considered a team leader. However, on the flip side of that, Dez Bryant can do the same thing, use the same words, and the media will brand him as an angry player. Even when the audio reveals that Dez Bryant was trying to motivate his team, people say the way he was doing it was not helpful. Why is the same thing not said about Tom Brady? Why does Dez Bryant lead the news when he shouts at his teammates, but Tom Brady does not, when he does the exact same thing?

What about Carson Palmer? He is a quarterback in the NFL who used to play for the Cincinnati Bengals. It has been well-documented and talked about that Carson Palmer wanted out of Cincinnati because he did not like the direction in which the organization was headed. He felt like they were not moving toward being better, so he wanted out of Cincinnati. He was commended for standing up for his beliefs and sticking to his guns. An interview was conducted where the head coach at the time, Marvin Lewis, said the QB and owner were both stubborn people and one of them had to remove themselves from the situation. Obviously, since it is the owner's team, Carson Palmer ended up leaving and finding another team in the NFL to play for. Now all that sounds fine—two people who had two different opinions, and in the end, a decision had to get made and it was made. However, imagine if this was a black athlete who had a problem with how an owner was running his organization. Think about all the black athletes who have had a problem with ownership, but instead were not handled with the grace of the Carson Palmer situation.

Another situation that demonstrates how the media treats black athletes differently from white athletes is Conor McGregor and Floyd Mayweather. Conor McGregor can say whatever he wants, talk trash about and to his opponents, talk about how much money he makes, and go on and on about how great he is, and the media loves it. However, if Floyd Mayweather talks about any of these things the media reports how arrogant he is. Mayweather has never lost a professional fight in his career, and he has made an astronomical amount of money for his fights. The fact that someone has actual facts and winnings to back up his statements, yet is treated so differently, leads me to wonder: Why is that when Floyd makes a comment, the media turns it around to a negative perspective? But when McGregor says anything, he is praised for "just being competitive and honest?" Floyd Mayweather retired being 49-0. That is 49 wins and zero losses. To clarify, can someone tell me, again, why he does not have the right to say something about his success? The media finds ways to make Mayweather's statements negative and untasteful. The truth is, Conor McGregor says and acts the same way, but he is given a flattering review. Those who interview him are often seen on television laughing along with him while he makes his rude comments. Some people reading this are going to say, "Yeah, but Floyd is a woman beater." I am sorry, but his being a woman beater and talking trash about his profession are two different things. Floyd is not the first athlete, and unfortunately will not be the last, to abuse a woman. I am not saying it is right, but I am saying do not get caught up in the ways the media makes it okay for you to talk negatively about Floyd, but praise McGregor.

This happens to female athletes as well. Let's look at Serena Williams, for example. She has dominated the world of Tennis since 1999, when she won her first Grand Slam title. She is, and has been, one of the best female athletes over the last 15+ years. She has not been caught up in any major scandals that have caused her to be suspended or lose endorsement deals like many other athletes. Yet, in the media, people talk about how her body looks "manly" and how she should not have so many muscles. There are pictures of her that get shown where viewers are able to comment on her body, even though this is the body that has allowed her to be as successful as she has been in her sport. She is not an average tennis player. In fact, many would say that she is the best tennis player in the world. Many consider the only person who stands in the way of Serena's success is Serena. Then, there is Ronda Rousey, who for many years, has been considered as the face of the women's UFC divisions. If you look at Ronda's body, it looks a lot like Serena's; it is extremely toned and refined. However, this is the way her body must be to sustain so much while fighting. However, why is Ronda Rousey's body not splashed on news channels with comments about how muscular she looks in different outfits? The only differences between these two highly successful woman athletes are the sports they participate in, and the color of their skin. Why is it more acceptable for Ronda to have muscles, but if Serena has them, people say that she "looks like a man?" This is the media influencing the viewers to see Serena as "more like a man." In turn, they plant the idea that her success is only because she has that advantage, and not because she has worked her tail off to get to where she is. Like all athletes, her body is a testament to that process.

Lastly, Ben Roethlisberger (this is going to be hard for me because I am a Steelers fan, but the truth is the truth) was accused two times of allegedly sexual assaulting a female. At the time it happened it was all over the news. People asked how this would impact his career, how the NFL would respond, and what would ultimately happen to Ben. However, over time the story died down. At one point, Ben stopped answering questions about the event in the news. Time went on, and he was suspended for the first four games of the next season. Eventually, all was forgotten. Yes, some people from rival teams and people who will never forget still bring it up on occasion. But the story has pretty much died down. What about Tiger Woods? He cheated on his wife with multiple women and that story was in the media for months. Each time a new woman came out, every media outlet replayed everything over and over again. The media went as far as showing graphics of timelines and where the women lived. There was even a chart on a media outlet that had in detail each woman as they came out and shared their story. Tiger Woods was the worst man on the planet for cheating on his wife, yet Ben still got to carry on being a leader of his team. Now, I am not and would not ever lessen what Tiger Woods did to his wife, but as a woman, I would rather be cheated on than assaulted. Of course the media however, clearly sees it differently. Again, the only differences between Ben and Tiger are the fact they play two different sports. Tiger Woods was married, and is black, Ben Roethlisberger is white. Tiger's indiscretions still get brought up, and I can tell you, as a Steelers fan who listens to all types of sports talk radio, Ben's indiscretions are not.

Media Agenda

It is important to think about the media's agenda and the story they want to portray. Unfortunately, they have audiences they are trying to win over and stories they need their viewers to be interested in. Because of this, they often have to sell the story by an image they put up on the screen or by saying things that keep you interested. But reporting the truth out of context leads me to believe that every news outlet has an agenda. For example, if you turn on various news channels and watch commercials, you can determine what kind of audience the channel is appealing to. If a car commercial plays, on a channel that is appealing to an audience with a high economic status, the cars that are advertised will be high-end cars like Jaguars, Range Rovers, etc. If a car commercial comes on for an audience with lower income, there will be more Chevy or Dodge commercials. The same way that advertisers separate their advertisements is the same way news channels segment their news in order to push their agendas.

There are two news outlets that I have fallen in love with over the past year because they deliver real news. Sometimes so real that I cringe while I am watching because they do not try to shelter their views on what is happening. They are not one-sided in delivering their news, and this benefits an audience who wants real news. Al Jeezera and RT are news outlet that not only share news about great things that happen in our world, but also giving voice and attention to stories that would not get much airtime or in depth news coverage on "mainstream media." This network is where you will see what happens in our black communities, the struggles with education, obtaining jobs, neighborhoods, and all the different experiences that happen to people of color. The bigger question is why CNN, MSNBC, FOX News, and other news outlets do not cover this as part of their daily stories, too? If anyone has the chance to create change and create conversation, it is our news channels. However, if they run stories about what is really happening in our black communities, then people would understand where the anger stems from. In turn, the understanding makes black struggles relevant. Black people do not roll out of bed angry, just like people of other races do not roll out of bed angry. But if we feel like we are being taken advantage of and not treated equally, we will be angry just like anyone would. If the media would show what the streets of Baltimore looked like on a daily basis and not just when black people are rioting, that would help change the perception of black people. The media has a hold over what people see and how they see it. They use their clout to influence how society sees and reacts to these stories.

If you believe the news you see on primetime news stations, you will think that in Africa there is only dirt, trees, and wild animals. Think about the last time you saw anywhere in Africa on the news with high rise hotels, gorgeous landscaping, and looked inviting? It probably has not happened because if the news showed the continent of Africa looking luxurious, then people would realize that black people deserve better treatment. By not showing how much Africa has to offer, it plays into the narrative that black people are less than, and unfortunately, a lot of people buy into this storyline.

Media Terminology

One thing the media excels in is telling stories the way they want to tell them regardless of how inconsistent the stories may be. Have you ever watched the news on mute and just looked at the people they have on the screen? Have you wondered about the wording they put under the person's name or facts that are under the person speaking? Have you ever paid attention to what quotes or what percentages are also under the subtitles? The message the media wants you to get is their message, not the actual message. Take for example, why is it that when a group of white people use guns to protect property they are called "militants." If a group of black people were involved in similar behavior they would be called "thugs" or "criminals." Sadly, Muslims using the same guns to protect their property would be labeled "terrorists." Why is it when people do the same things, but they have different skin color or religious affiliations, their actions are seen differently or even as harmful?

The media is responsible for putting out terminology that fits the story they want to tell. This is, of course, needs to stay in line with the standards that society has in place. This accidental knowledge the media talks about and displays are things that people latch onto, and before you know it, the media plants seeds in our minds that grow over time. When people see percentages and statistics, they believe the numbers are actually facts. This is an issue because percentages and statistics can be skewed based on where the data come from. For an example, if a story says 63% of African Americans are more likely to be on welfare than whites, that number sounds staggering. However, in order to correctly interpret that "information," we need more details: did the data come from one neighborhood, one city, or one region? Who were the respondents? How can we be sure the survey accurately represented anything? When listening to the media you always have to ask yourself additional questions about where they got this number from, where the survey was conducted, who are the people that took the survey, and how did they confirm these numbers as affirmative data? There are a lot more questions that can be asked, but these are the basics and if we do not have answers to these questions, it is extremely hard to know if the numbers reported by the media are accurate. Paying attention to what the media does not say is more important than listening to the words they do say.

Conclusion

These are examples that show the media treats or reports on black people differently from others. Think about for a second who is asking the interview questions? Who comes up with the storyline, and what type of person pulls the strings behind the scenes? Whether it is regular news or sports news, these stations have to run through what they will say in order to make sure they are "speaking to their audience." This is what creates the problem because the media skews the story to appeal to their audience. If this did not happen, you would see the real people behind the stories and how they live on a daily basis, not just what the media wants you to see. Still, not convinced? Try to Google "Fault Lines Al Jazeera" or "RT documentaries about inequality." I promise you the stories you see on these will not reflect what we are being shown on a daily basis. Think about the news we do not see; the real stories and struggles the news could report on that are honest, but might not fit into their narrative. Shaping the news to fit a narrative that is in line with a perspective of people, even if that narrative is wrong, attracts and keeps viewers. It will still show what is happening in this country and in areas that are often neglected are written off.

Either you deal with what is the reality, or you can be sure that the reality is going to deal with you.

~ Alex Haley

Three

THE BLACK STRUGGLE

...to the flag

S tandards, when it comes to black people, have gotten out of control. It seems like when a black person does something that is not considered "normal," the person committing the action gets scrutinized. The Green Bay Packers QB, Aaron Rodgers, used to celebrate after every touchdown he scored by acting like he was putting a championship belt around his waist. His celebration was talked about so much that State Farm decided to endorse him to include that celebration as part of their marketing strategy. Fast forward to Cam Newton, who decided to "dab" every time he gets into the end zone, and it created backlash. People began to say things like:

1. "He should not be celebrating this much."
2. "Why does he have this individual celebration, why is he not celebrating with his team?"
3. "Cam Newton is taunting his opponents."

Both men play the exact same position, and they both decided they wanted to do something special when they got in the end zone. However, of the two, only one man gets criticized for it. There is only one difference between Cam Newton and Aaron Rodgers, and that is their race. People he said Cam Newton was taking the spotlight away from his team and he was a terrible leader. Aaron Rodgers, on the other hand, collected checks for the same type of behavior.

It is these inequities that cause misperceptions of black people, and make the actions of a white athlete greater than the actions of a black athlete. These athletes play the same position and choose to celebrate when they get in the end zone. Yet, one athlete is criticized, while another is celebrated. Unfortunately, this is not the only example of inequities that black people are faced with. For some reason anything that is not of the "norm," as deemed by society, can cause people who participate in abnormal behaviors to be perceived as the ones who are doing something wrong.

Guilty of Being.....

Not too long ago, a young black teen wearing a hoodie was shot to death because a civilian thought that he looked suspicious. Never mind the fact that it was raining, he was black and he was wearing a hoodie. Because of this, the man decided to follow the child through the neighborhood. Of course the teen was also walking through an upscale neighborhood, and based on these factors, the civilian decided that he was out of place. The ridiculous part of this story is the African American teen was trying to go back to his home since he lived in the neighborhood. There are so many things wrong with this situation, but a few things that are undeniable are that a civilian saw a black man, wearing a hoodie in a neighborhood where the civilian assumed a black person did not live in, so therefore, the teen must have been doing some wrong.... Right?

Black people always have to make sure they are in a location where they "fit" because if not, they are subject to be accused of things they are not doing, or have people thinking their intentions are not pure. In the example above, we will never know if it was the hoodie, being black, being in a particular neighborhood, or some combination of these that motivated the civilian to follow the teen. But whatever the reason, none of those things helped the civilian's perceptions of the teen. All my life, I have heard people say, "Perception is reality." The truth is that perception is only reality based on what kind of perception you have. Because if the reality is that black people can live in upscale communities, and they can wear hoodies without being criminals, it disrupts the stereotypical narrative of black people that exists in society. More importantly, someone can be black and not commit a crime. The simple fact of being black does not mean he/she is doing anything illegal. The same goes for baggy pants, since the reality is that anyone can wear baggy pants. However, wearing them does not make you a criminal or any less of a person. There have been countless white people who have worn baggy pants, including celebrities, athletes, and normal people who are not perceived as criminals. So why do black people have to go through life with these standards and perceptions placed on them when others do not?

Black Men Speaking their Mind

There have been several instances where black people have spoken up about inequities or stated facts about the life they have experienced. Sadly, for those who do speak up, people usually try to make them seem like what they are talking about is crazy. If it is a celebrity, people act like they just do not understand what black people are going through because they are rich. If it is a politician, people act like they have lost touch with reality because of their status. If it is someone who does not have any accolades, it is a knock on their experience or where they are getting their information. What people seem to forget is when a black man is speaking, 9 times out of 10 he is speaking about something he has personally experienced. Like others, he has opinions about what he sees happening in the world, or ways that he feels things can be better for his community. Now granted, not every single black person was raised in the ghetto, brought up without parents, or struggled through life. But being a black person, you know someone who has, and if you have not experienced it yourself, that is where these thoughts and ideas start. They might not be popular thoughts, but they are indeed true. If a black man says something, people rush to discredit the statement. Why, you might ask? Because it minimizes the problems and issues we face as black people. This is a way to oppress an opinion that is not popular, even though the comments speak a lot of truth.

Richard Sherman, Kanye West, and Malcolm X come to mind when I think about black men who speak or have spoken their minds. They are three men who immediately pop out. Obviously, there are a lot more black men who let the world know their thoughts, but these three are current and memorable. For those of you that do not know, Richard Sherman plays football in the NFL, Kanye West is an artist, and Malcolm X was a human rights activist. One thing each of these men have in common is they do not apologize for the things they say. In fact, listening to the things they have said makes people uncomfortable. In turn, it makes these men seem defiant, even though they are speaking their truths.

Richard Sherman was first recognized as being outspoken when he had a microphone shoved in his face after he made a game-ending deflection against a receiver that helped his team get to the Super Bowl in 2014. When he had the microphone in his face he made some comments about a player on the opposing team in a negative light, and he also commented about himself as a player. However, because of what he said about the person on the opposing team, that was the sound bite that was played all over the news. Since his team was going to the Super Bowl, in the weeks leading up to it, he was constantly interviewed and reporters continued to try and get the best sound bites from Sherman that they could. What actually happened was Richard Sherman saying factual and unpopular comments in his interviews. A few of his quotes include:

1. "I'm intelligent enough and capable enough to understand that you are an ignorant, pompous, egotistical, cretin. I'm going to

crush you on here because I'm tired of hearing about it." - To Skip Bayless

2. "I think people somehow get a skewed view of Tom Brady. That he's just a clean-cut guy that does everything right and never says a bad word to anyone. We know him to be otherwise. - About Tom Brady

The reason why these two quotes were being highlighted was because he was commenting on a man who continuously talked about. Tom Brady was seen as the Golden Boy of the NFL, and in turn, made Richard Sherman sound unfavorable when he spoke out against him. However, it was because Richard Sherman saw Tom Brady as a different type of person, and he was speaking out about it. It was comments like these that, in Sherman's perspective and a lot of other people's perspectives, made the media portray Sherman as a man who was "off his rocker," making baseless comments. We do not know what Richard Sherman goes through or the things that he deals with, but because he made combative comments, he was labeled as a thug, outrageous, combative, and uneducated. Here are my issues with that. Richard Sherman graduated from Stanford University with a degree in communications. The majority of us would never get into Stanford, but here he is—a black man who beat all the odds, and now he has a platform and a voice to express the way he feels. How could be considered uneducated and out of touch because he was stating how he felt?

Kanye West is an artist who never holds back his thoughts. However, because his thoughts, on the surface, seem to be off the wall, people always try to put Kanye in a box that has him labeled as "crazy" or "delusional." But by doing this, the message that Kanye is trying to deliver often goes un-noticed. Personally, since Kanye's mother passed away, maybe we can say he is more off the wall than usual. But the things that he says are not crazy or confusing when you actually look at the context in which he is making his statements. In 2005 during a live fundraiser for Hurricane Katrina, Kanye West said, "George Bush does not like black people." At the time, many people were criticizing and questioning former President Bush's actions on his handling of the disaster. People wondered why they were not warned in a timely manner, and what was taking help so long to arrive. It seemed like he was not taking what happened seriously. However, once pictures came out and people were outraged by how much devastation there actually was, then former President Bush reacted. At the time of the live fundraiser, there were a ton of conversations in the media about how things were being handled and if Bush was doing enough to help the people in New Orleans. Some media outlets raised the question if Bush would have reacted differently had the city been one that was populated with rich people? At any rate, with all of this going around, the live fundraiser was televised and Kanye West made his statements. If you look at everything that was happening at the time, Kanye was not the only person that felt that way. Many black people felt the same way, but Kanye was able to be on a stage and in a position to actually state his feelings.

Kanye has also been known for publicly disagree with Taylor Swift receiving the Album of the Year Award over Beyoncé. The truth is, a lot of people agreed with Kanye that Beyoncé should have won that award. There have been other times where he criticized the choices of other awards shows because he did not agree with, or understand how, they made their decisions. More recently, Kanye has gone on "Twitter rants," which often included statements where he spoke out about everything under the sun. His topics covered his artistry, success, visions, struggles, relationships, and his past. Some people think what he is saying is so far off the wall that he has to be crazy. Well no, not really. If you look at Kanye's tweets, he is expressing himself and speaking about things that are important to him. Unfortunately, people take 5 or 6 tweets Kanye says, patch them together, throw in the fact that he is married to a Kardashian, and assume that he is not making sense. By doing this to him, it discredits everything that he is trying to say. I have listened to a dozen interviews Kanye has done and read several interviews that he has given. A lot of the things that he says are extremely accurate. They are raw, unedited, and very straight forward. But they are factual. Instead, if people would try reading his tweets to understand what he says in its context, they would be less likely to discredit him so quickly.

If Kanye can be made out to look like a crazy man who was just talking about things that were untrue, his messages will get lost. On a bigger scale of things, what if more black people supported Kanye outwardly and starting being more supportive of his comments and beliefs? His potential has the power to play a role in creating a revolution for black people. It is important for us to not only take note, but to take action in situations that hold us back. Are the things that Kanye says really that controversial, dumb, un-grounded, and not thought out? No, I do not believe so. They might not always be said at the right time, but his timing is based on his opportunities and he takes full advantage of them.

Malcolm X was another controversial man who is obviously more a part of our history since he is no longer living. As stated before, Malcolm X was a human rights activist who, depending on who you ask, was considered either a radical or someone that consistently spoke his truth and stuck to his convictions. No matter how you view Malcolm X, he was someone who spoke his mind. There was nothing that was off limits when it came to Malcolm X. He was raised in a time when black people were not treated or seen as equal people. He often spoke from a place of trying to empower black people to allow them to be more aware of what was happening in their communities. He did not want black people as a group to allow themselves to fall victim to their circumstances. Malcolm X was focused on the black community because every day he saw the inequities and struggles that people were dealing with. He wanted black people to overcome the things they were going through.

There is so much literature out there about Malcolm X, so instead of telling his story, I want to focus on some of his quotes that show how him speaking his mind was considered a red flag. Even though his statements were an accurate reflection of his experiences, oddly enough, a lot of his quotes still ring true today. In my mind, this indicates just how far we really are from having everyone treated equally. Below are four quotes that illustrate how outspoken he was, how he tried to urged other people to no longer be a victim of their circumstances, and how he encouraged black people to take action to becoming a better version of themselves.

1. "*They put your mind right in a bag, and take it wherever they want.*"
2. "*A race of people is like an individual man; until it uses its own talent, takes pride in its own history, expresses its own culture, affirms its own selfhood, it can never fulfill itself.*"
3. "*I believe that there will ultimately be a clash between the oppressed and those that do the oppressing. I believe that there will be a clash between those who want freedom, justice and equality for everyone and those who want to continue the systems of exploitation.*"
4. "*You can't separate peace from freedom because no one can be at peace unless he has his freedom.*" — *Malcolm X*

In the first quote, he felt like if you do not think for yourself, you are allowing people to take whatever they want from you. Similarly, the second quote relates to black people taking ownership of who they are so that you can truly reach your potential. The last two focus on how he felt black people felt about the justice system and how having freedom is liberating. Remember Malcolm X was concerned for black people and their futures as individuals. Each of these quotes is a very honest and open assessment of things that, as black people, we need to realize if we ever want to accomplish our goals. In essence, he was trying to educate black people to be better, ask more questions, and pay attention. He was also directing this toward white people and anyone he felt was playing a part in hindering the forward movement of black people. The Malcolm X movie is a brilliant illustration of who he was and how black and white people perceived him. It is worth noting that perception is pretty similar to things that are happening today.

When you look at all three of these men, they each in their own right are bold, outspoken, and communicate with a purpose. They are not just making up things to say. They speak truths and give insightful information in order to force change. For the record, I am by no means comparing these three men to each other, but merely stating the fact that they each speak on topics that people are uncomfortable talking about. Therefore, sometimes because they speak out openly and controversially, people try to discredit what they are saying even though they are speaking the truth.

Lastly, why does someone being outspoken make us uncomfortable? Why don't we ask ourselves, why this is making us uncomfortable? As a society, we need to start conversations about things that make us uncomfortable. That is how we grow as people, and that is how we will become more understanding of each other. The message these men convey is correct. We need to stop scrutinizing and downplaying black men when they speak up or when they occupy a position of power. We need to pay attention to, and understand the message that is being conveyed. It is also important to apply what people say about situations when it comes to your circumstances. Just because a black man says something does not mean he is saying out of anger or aggression. He could actually be speaking factual information, and his skin tone should not become a factor in discrediting his words.

Thug New Word for Nigger

For some reason in today's society when ANY black person seems to be aggressive, angry, behave a certain way, or make comments that might not be popular, they get labeled. That label is almost always "thug." I am sure many of you are aware that back during slavery, black people were called all sorts of things, including "monkey," "coon," and "nigger"— just to name the first three that come to mind. In today's day and age, those names are considered derogatory, so people tend to shy away from using any of them. However, the word "thug" has begun to be used by various people trying to find a way to label a black person. An example of this would be when Richard Sherman made his comments after a competitive NFL playoff game. In the days following, the word people used to describe him was "thug." To drive my point home, I looked in four different places for definitions of thug:

1. **Google Search:** A violent person, especially a criminal. Some synonyms that were identified; ruffian, hooligan, vandal, hoodlum, gangster, villain, criminal.
2. **Historical Definition**: A member of a religious organization of robbers and assassins in India. Devotees of the goddess Kali, the Thugs waylaid and strangled their victims, usually travelers, in a ritually prescribed manner. They were suppressed by the British in the 1830s.
3. **Urban Dictionary**: A thug is someone who is going through struggles, has gone through struggles, and continues to live day by day with nothing for them. That person is a thug. The life they are living is the thug life.
4. **Merriam Dictionary**: A brutal ruffian or assassin

Based on each of these definitions, not one thing that Richard Sherman did classified him as a "thug," but one thing that he is, is black. For some reason, black people who act a certain way have to be given a label. They cannot just be expressing themselves; they have to be called something, and since the terms I stated earlier are now inappropriate, the next best word to use is "thug." However, it is only used on black people, just like the word "nigger" used to be. We do not need more proof that men, such as Johnny Manziel, Justin Bieber, Scott Disick, Dylann Roof, and James Eagan Holmes are all white men who have acted in ways similar to black men who have been labeled as "thugs." It is no media secret that these men have been in the news for partying too much, who do not take their responsibilities seriously, make bad decisions, and even kill people. However, they have not been labeled as thugs. Excuses were made for them. They were not labeled as thugs because of circumstances, mental illness, or numerous other reasons (excuses).

Essentially black people are labeled based on what they wear, look like, act like, how they talk, dress, stand, and walk. It seems that anything you can think of allows us to be labeled, and at any minute, if we do something that can be taken as "aggressive," we are called thugs. Don't believe me? For 30 seconds, let's think about some labels that are put on white people. As I write this book, I cannot think of one. For blacks, it is not the same story. For some reason, we have to be put in a category, and almost always, it is a way to make sure we can be identified. Once we are identified as good, then we are alright to put up with. But if we are identified as a "thug," then it is alright to be discarded. The problem here is why we need to be identified or classified as anything to begin with. We are aware that we are black, and we are reminded of it every day and through every situation we encounter.

The word "thug" has to be taken out of our vocabulary as a way to explain black people. It is a derogatory term just like all other terms that are used to identify groups of people. Everywhere that I have been, whether for personal or professional reasons, I have heard people use the word "thug" to describe a black person they deemed as less than, or not looking the part. How many times have you heard the word thug being used to describe a white person who was acting aggressively? Think about that for a second. Why are we using this word to describe blacks? "Thug" does not equal black people, and the more times it gets used to describe black people, the closer we get to separating an entire race of people through a dangerous term. Some people say, "You are dressed like a thug today" or "You look like a thug." What does this mean? That a person looks like a criminal or sloppy? Every black person in a hoodie does not equal to a thug, or does not mean that that person is doing something wrong. Once we can start seeing people for who they are and not judging them based on skin tone, we can bridge some gaps that have continuously created barriers for black people.

Oppression

Unfortunately, when speaking about black people the topic of oppression has be brought up. The sad part of being oppressed is that it has been happening since slavery. For those of you who do not know, being oppressed can be highlighted by injustices and suffering. Everything already discussed presents a solid example of how black people are oppressed on a daily basis. Other areas include education and housing. Why is it considered normal to have children attending a school where all the toilets do not work and the roofs are leaking? What about housing and neighborhoods being run down and money not going back into these environments to make things better? Similarly, everything else that will be discussed in this book identifies ways in which black people are oppressed. Just because on the outside it seems like things have gotten better, does not mean that people in society are not contributing to the suffering in society since we all play a role in what is happening.

Now some people will say that black people are responsible for their own oppression, and they will accredit their ideas to what they have seen on television or what they have programmed themselves to believe. Again, if you are this person, think about your life and the privileges you have. Do you think it is fun or exciting for black people to go through this oppression? Yes, we are responsible for acquiescing to the low standards given to us, but we are not responsible for being born into certain situations and not having the right resources to help make our situation better. Some people will get confused with the success that is seen in the media of black people, and they assume all black people should be able to live up to these standards, but that is not true. The media's job is to promote stories and give people information they are interested in. However, the reality is famous people are not representative of the black population. It is time to start looking at our black communities and black people who are average human beings. They have struggles of oppression every day and do not have the money or the resources to get themselves out of their situations. Nobody wants to be oppressed, and if oppression is ever going to stop, black people CONSISTENTLY have to be given equal opportunities and resources.

Conclusion

When you have certain standards and perceptions that you arbitrarily apply to a group of people, you immediately put them at a disadvantage. Why can black people not get the benefit of the doubt? Why do we have these perceptions about us even when our intentions are good? The answer is, society has taught people these perceptions, and we do not even realize they are embedded in the ways we act and the things that are said. Why does someone being uncomfortable mean that someone is deviant? I want to be able to express myself just like anyone else can. Almost every day, if not every day, before I act on something or make a comment, I have to remind myself that I am black. This causes me to think about how I want to say things and consider how they will impact someone else. I am about 95% sure that I am not the only black person who thinks this way. I talk loud and sound aggressive, and I can promise you that I am nowhere close to being a thug by definition, or a thug by society's definition. But if I react the wrong way or do the wrong thing, that label will immediately be tied to me, only because I am a black woman.

Hatred paralyzes life; love releases it. Hatred confuses life; love harmonizes it. Hatred darkens life; love illuminates it.

~ Martin Luther King, Jr.

Four

THE SPORTS WORLD

...of the United States of America

It is hard for me to look beyond the game in order to look deeper into what is happening in sports. We have to remember that inequities occur within sports, but often they are overshadowed by what the media wants you to think about. Further, for teams they deem important, their stories are the ones they want to bring to the forefront. However, we all know the stories that are put on the radio, TV, or newspapers are not the only part of the story that is actually happening. The issue of race can often times go undetected in sports because so many athletes at all levels of sports are indeed black. But there are inequities in sports that happen a lot of the time.

Why are there not more black head coaches of professional teams? Black coaches are often good enough to be the "best assistant" coaches around, but when it comes to them being in charge of an entire team, why are they not good enough for that job? What about the players who get good publicity versus the ones who get bad publicity? What about salaries? Besides quarterbacks, who have historically been white, how many times do we hear how much money white players are getting paid after contract negotiations? Almost every time a black player signs a deal with a large sum of money, the media is all over it, tweeting, interviewing, and writing articles about the dollar amounts. Why is that? There are white players who play professionally; why aren't their contracts highlighted? Now, MLB does a better job at letting the fans know their players' salaries regardless of race. The NFL and NBA, however, fall short of this. What will be highlighted in this chapter are the inequities that are experienced in sports and how it happens so often, it is seen as normal.

Black Coaches in the NFL

The question that was asked earlier about how can a coach be such a great assistant coach, but not be good enough to be a head coach comes with this reality. The reality is, there are white coaches who fail just like black coaches. However, the white coaches often continue to get chance after chance to be successful. Currently, Jeff Fisher is in his 3rd head coaching job (if you factor in that he was with the Houston Oilers who then moved and became the Tennessee Titans), and has been a coach in the NFL for about 20 years. In his first season he took over the team that he is currently coaching, and he was 7-8-1 in 2012, after being 2-14 the previous years at his previous organization, the Tennessee Titans. In years following 2012, he was 7-9, 6-10, and 7-9 in the 2015 season. Although he has shown some signs of improvement since he first took over the team, they are not much more improved over the past few years. Nonetheless, every year sport analysts say "this year should be their breakout year." Previously, Jeff Fisher was a head coach from 1994 season through 2010. He has made the playoffs and even had a chance to coach in a Super Bowl, where he lost by inches. Overall, in his last 7 seasons with the Tennessee Titans he is 54-58. That record, and his coaching were still good enough to land him the job for the St. Louis Rams, which is now the Los Angeles Rams. There have been other coaches who have been given similar opportunities. Rex Ryan, Chip Kelly, Jack Del Rio, and Gary Kubiak are the most recent head coaches who have been fired from one job and almost immediately landed a new head coaching job.

On the flip side, black coaches are not as lucky. Mike Singletary coached the San Francisco 49ers between 2008 and 2010 seasons, and during that time he was 18-22. Since 2010, he has not been offered a head coaching job. Hue Jackson was 8-8 in 2011, and after one season in Oakland, he was fired and just got his next head coaching job for the 2016 season. In addition, Lovie Smith coached nine seasons, was 81-63, and was fired after a 10-6 season. He got another chance two years later and was 2-14 one season and 6-10 the next season, and he was fired with his total record being 89-87. I have put a chart below to compare these coaches side by side with their win records for more clarification:

Mike Singletary: 8 - 22
Hue Jackson: 8 - 8
Lovie Smith: 89 - 87
Chip Kelly: 26 - 21
Jack Del Rio: 76 - 82
Gary Kubiak: 73 - 68
Rex Ryan: 54 - 58

Just by looking at these numbers you can tell that white coaches are given more opportunities than black coaches. Remember it is not about the number of coaches that are used for this illustration, it is about the number of opportunities the white coaches have gotten and continue to get!

The white coaches have a combined career record of 398 -385, while the black coaches have a 105 - 117 combined career. These higher numbers go to show that white coaches continue to get jobs and have more opportunities to reach their dreams than black coaches. It should also be noted that Jeff Fisher and Lovie Smith have both been to a Super Bowl and lost, whereas Gary Kubiak went to and won the Super Bowl for the 2015 season. Now, what would be the reason why white head coaches would be given more opportunities than black coaches? Mike Singletary and Hue Jackson both were good enough to be assistant coaches. Why were they not given another opportunity? Could we say that race played a factor? Of course, we could also say maybe they were not good head coaches, but, the same thing can be said for the white coaches. Yet they continue to get jobs. Currently, Mike Tomlin, Marvin Lewis, Todd Bowles, and Jim Caldwell are the only five black head coaches in the NFL, which is about 15% of the NFL, despite the fact that roughly 69% of players in the NFL are black players.

No matter how many articles are written, or how much attention gets paid to this topic, things do not change. There is currently a Rooney Rule in the NFL that forces organizations to interview black coaches for head coaching jobs. If everything was fair and they were being considered, why do we need a Rooney Rule? Coaching jobs should be about who is qualified to do the job and should not be determined by race. However, by having this rule, it is obvious that these organizations do not view black coaches as good enough to be their head coaches. Mike Tomlin and Tony Dungy have proven that black coaches can be successful because each of these coaches have been to a total of four Super Bowls. Each of them has taken their team to two Super Bowls, and each has won one. This is proof that success can happen with a black coach, so now the question is, when will black coaches be given the opportunities to prove they can interview for jobs effectively and be successful at being a head coach? Remember this is not just happening in the NFL. The MLB and NBA also have a shortage of black coaches.

Black Men in Professional Sports

For years there have been debates, articles written, and conversations around black men in sports. This is an interesting topic because in some sports there are more black people than any other race. As mentioned before, the NFL and NBA are the two biggest organizations that have black male athletes involved. Track would be another sport that potentially has more blacks than any other race. Within those sports, there are several black athletes and coaches who have been successful based on the opportunities they have been given. However, black players and coaches are often on a shorter leash, get judged harsher, and have lose opportunities more readily if they do not perform on a consistent basis. As talked about before, this happens with head coaching jobs in the NFL, but that is not the only way that black men are treated differently.

COACHES

Mark Jackson was the coach of the Golden State Warriors prior to the Warriors winning the NBA finals for the 2014-2015 season. Currently, in 2016, the Warriors are arguably the best team in the NBA and have a chance to win another championship. However, when people talk about the Golden State Warriors' success, they do not mention Mark Jackson being an integral part of building the team. Almost all the core players who have been a part of the Warriors' successes have come from the players that Mark Jackson selected for the team. Now, is Mark Jackson the *only* reason why the team won a championship after he left? Absolutely not. But you cannot deny the role he played in getting the team on the right track to win a championship. Of course now, Steve Kerr is the coach of the Golden State Warriors and for those of you who do not know, he is a white man.

Tony Dungy is another black coach who was let go as the coach of a team, and the very next year the team he left went on to win a Super Bowl. Similar to Mark Jackson, Tony Dungy played a large role into getting the team on track and making them a team that was cohesive. The very next year Jon Gruden was hired as the head coach and he won a Super Bowl with a lot of the same players that Tony Dungy had. Again, all the credit was given to Jon Gruden about how great of a coach he was and how he played such an integral part in the Tampa Bay Buccaneers winning the Super Bowl. Where was the credit for Tony Dungy?

With each of these cases, a black man was fired from his job and the next year when a white coach took over his position, they won a championship. Is it coincident that this happened? Possibly. But the ironic reality is that it did happen, and in both cases, it was the black coach who missed out on achieving this goal. We will never know if Mark Jackson or Tony Dungy would have won a championship if they were still the coaches. But what we do know is they were not given any credit for laying a solid foundation and bringing players to the team that would ultimately help with their success. On the flip side of that, Jim E. Mora and Bill Cowher were the coaches of the Indianapolis Colts and Pittsburgh Steelers, respectively. After they left their organizations, their replacement head coaches, Tony Dungy and Mike Tomlin, who are both black won Super Bowls. In these instances, the conversation in the media was how much of an imprint the former Colts and Steelers coaches had on the teams that won championships. In other words, when a black coach wins it, it is the "white coach's imprint" that helped him to do so. When the white coach wins after the black coach leaves, nobody mentions the role the black coach played in that win. Why does this happen?

Coaches Gregg Popovich and Bill Belichick are known for being two coaches who hate talking to the media. The reasons why they hate it are the reasons why anyone would: being asked repetitive questions, questions that have obvious answers, and being disturbed when your team is trying to prepare for a game. These issues are even worse after they lose a game or while a game is in process. However, the media is a part of the job, and it is something that has to be done. These two coaches have gotten out of answering questions and dealing with the media by giving short answers that illustrate how annoyed they are with the media instead of answering questions. This has become their signature way of doing interviews—so much so that people expect them to be that way. When a black coach does an interview and they give short answers, the media person will often ask them to explain their answer. This often results in the coaches giving more detail, which leads to more questions. Sometimes this leads to getting off topic and the coach making a headlining statement. These kinds of statements are taken and plastered on websites and headlines for news stations. Does this happen all the time with every interview? No. But the real question is why does it ever happen? Why is it alright for some coaches to answer questions the way they want to and others get pressed for doing so? Whether race actually plays a factor in this or not, it cannot be ignored that white coaches are given more privileges. Why don't reporters push Popovich and Belichick? Better yet, how can the NBA or the NFL stop this from happening? The media is part of the job, and it comes with being a player or coach. It baffles my mind why some coaches get away with answering questions the way they do, and others do not.

Players

For athletes, their experiences are similar to the coaches. But unfortunately, when a player is no longer given opportunities, it means that they are out of the business or they have to scrounge around for opportunities. A coach can go from being a head coach to various other types of coaching. For players, when their time is up and nobody wants to give them another opportunity, they essentially need to change their careers. Black athletes are the majority of this type of group when it comes to the NFL, but when you look at black athletes by position, it is the quarterback position that is most vulnerable to this type of treatment for black players. In the past 5 years, there have been white quarterbacks who have continuously been able to get starting jobs and get paid a lot of money in the process. But the same cannot be said about black quarterbacks. Matt Flynn, Sam Bradford, Matt Cassel, Ryan Fitzpatrick, and Bryan Hoyer are all white quarterbacks who have had opportunities to lead multiple teams, and all of them combined have had two playoff appearances, both resulting in losses. On the opposite side of this, you have Robert Griffin III and Colin Kaepernick, two black quarterbacks who have both been to the playoffs. Kaepernick went to a Super Bowl, and the year after, was a pass deflection away to going back again.

Both have proven they can lead their teams to success, but organizations are hesitant to give them another shot. Again, this begs the question: Why do obviously more athletic and proven quarterbacks get overlooked, yet white quarterbacks who have not proven themselves at all continue to get large contracts thrown their way? I am sure there can be several excuses to why this is happening, but one thing you cannot deny is success. These black quarterbacks have been successful, and yet, they are still being treated like they are "average." Yes, Robert Griffin III did eventually get a shot to go to the Browns. However, this was on a one-year deal, and they still drafted a quarterback in the first round. As for Colin Kaepernick, a team wanted him, but he was going to have to take a pay cut in order to move. Once again, white quarterbacks are given certain privileges and black quarterbacks are not. Unfortunately, they are still expected to lead their teams to Super Bowls.

College Sports

College sports has become an industry where The National Collegiate Athletic Association or NCAA is making billions of dollars for putting kids on television to play their respectful sports. While college sports are enjoyable and some would even say more enjoyable to than professional sports, these athletes are being used as cash cows. The NCAA has television deals with the likes of ESPN, TBS, ABC, CBS, and other conference networks in order to have their games televised on national television. This sounds great, but even though the NCAA is making billions off of the product they put on television, the players do not receive any of this money and are, in many ways, free labor. Unfortunately, from the outside looking in, these kids look like they are living a life of privilege. They are student athletes, and they get a lot of attention. They have money to go to school and special treatment such as being given food, clothes, and other perks of being a student athlete. However, what does not get publicized as much is the amount of time they have to spend practicing for their sports, as well as the things they miss out on because they are athletes. Not to mention how they get treated as essentially employees by their athletic programs, but they do not get any direct monetary payments.

For those of you who do not know, student athletes have 20 hours a week they can use for sports related activities. That is 20 hours on top of their customary responsibilities of being a student and having a college experience. Imagine being in college and spending more time with your coaches and teammates than you get to spend on other college activities. It also needs to be mentioned that not every single college athlete has similar privileges. If you are a star of the team or someone that has high potential, you are given more privileges and greater leniency than some of the other players. This is where a lot of the inequities begin.

ATHLETES

Over the past 15 years, there have been a ton of scandals that have happened in the NCAA, and they have involved athletes and their coaches and staffs. We now know that these programs allowed their student athletes to take classes that either did not exist, or classes that were made up and given false grades. This might seem like a perk for these student athletes, but let's look at the population of these student athletes. In the revenue- generating sports, such as basketball and football, the athletes are predominately black. These athletes are not even getting educated at the schools they attend. If they are not getting educated, then they are not learning valuable life lessons, and they are not getting degrees for attending school. Who does this negatively impact? Black student athletes. The reality is, less than 1% of ALL student athletes will go pro. So the chances of a sport becoming a viable way to make money goes out the door for 99% of these students. Why does this matter? Since there is a majority amount of black student athletes, that is a majority of black people who are going to school and not getting educated; the system is failing them. This is the very system they are dedicating all their time and giving all of their energy toward, and the schools are not even helping them in their lives. We can say that the students have a responsibility to make sure that they get their education, but what about the responsibility of the coaches and the athletic departments? As a 19-23 year old student, the majority of us would take the easy way out and not ask any questions. At that age, you do not realize how much an education will help you in your life. In fact, it is up to the coaches to respect these student athletes enough to help them make decisions that will benefit their future. However, what happens is that these coaches and athletic departments are more worried about getting their athletes to play and making them eligible—so much so that the services they give them are ignored. The athletic system that is supposed to provide support and guidance to these young adults is the same system that takes away their ability to use college as a stepping stone to flourish as successful adults.

NCAA

Some of you are probably wondering, well why does this even matter and what does this have to do with black people getting unfair treatment? It is simple, this athletic system is set up in a way where white people, in power, make all the decisions and make a lot of money off these black athletes who do not reap any rewards. As stated before, not that many student athletes go pro and a lot of them do not get an education. The NCAA should be responsible for the standards they set for their programs. For example, if they decided to put in a rule where 85% of student athletes in every sport must graduate college with a Bachelor's degree, these student athletes would benefit from their hard work. But the way the systems are set up, the NCAA makes money off these athletes and when their four years of eligibility are up, that is it. Billions of dollars are made off of them and their talents, but they do not see the money, do not have a degree to show for it, and in most cases, they do not know what to do with their lives once their sport comes to an end. When you have a black dominated environment, where these students are essentially being used to make money to support the less than 1% who will go on to professional sports careers, it is an issue.

In Division I athletics, the bigger schools have 85% of people in positions of authority in athletics who are white. Similarly, the leadership and people making decisions on behalf of the NCAA are about 80% white. It is obvious whose interests these decision makers have in mind when they make rules for these athletes to follow. Just imagine, what if athletes were compensated for the amount of money they made for the NCAA? The NCAA could create a rule that indicated that the athletes could receive a certain percentage while they are in school, and once they graduate, they would able to get the rest of the money. Either way, this would mean that the people who are responsible for putting money in the bank accounts and pockets of the people who make decisions for the NCAA would also benefit from their hard work.

In a previous chapter book I wrote about slavery and how in a lot of ways slavery still happens. The reality is, the NCAA is a big part of the slavery that is happening to these college students. The schools and organizations profit from people who do not receive any monetary benefits and who are also restricted from going on and making side money or additional money on their own. Just like in slavery, the NCAA and the athletic departments' own the rights to these student athletes and limit their abilities to make money on their own. The NCAA and athletic department are slave owners, and these black student athletes are unfortunately paying the price.

Conclusion

Sports is just another example of how black people are treated differently from whites. Yes, there are more examples than what I referred to, but I wanted to focus on things that were in the news and situations that were easily searchable. We live in a world where people will always want to discredit or disprove anything that is written and chalk it up to something other than what actually happens. The facts are the facts, and although it is hard to consider the sports we love to not be fair, that is what is happening. Black people in all situations have to worry about getting judged by the color of their skin. Sports provides exciting moments and does create a lot of great learning opportunities. That does not mean that race does not play a factor when key decisions are made. If you are still not a believer, what other reason is there for black coaches and players to get treated differently compared to their white counterparts?

*The way to right wrongs is to turn the
light of truth upon them.*

~ Ida B. Wells

Five

EDUCATION

...and to the Republic

G rowing up I knew the importance of education and the benefits that it could potentially bring for my life. As a former student athlete, it was constantly embedded in me that without good grades, continuing to play volleyball would not be an option. From the time I was a kid, until I finished my bachelor's degree, I was not the best student. Admittedly, I did just enough to pass, but never more than that. It was not until I entered the workforce and got a job (that I did not want to do) that I realized the benefits of school. Now let me be clear, I always set a goal for myself to get my PhD, because initially, I wanted to be a psychologist. Being in the workforce after college and working a job to pay the bills, just to make ends meet, was not a goal of mine. However, I knew that if I wanted to put myself in a better situation where I was not working to just pay bills, education is what was going to put me on that path.

After understanding what I wanted from my life, school, for me, was always a place to go to for comfort. School became a place where my friends were and the place where pushing myself was necessary. It was not until the beginning of getting my Master's degree where I began looking at school a little differently. Looking back on it now, I am not sure if it was because I was mature in age, but now, I feel that various other things made me start to see education differently. I started questioning the messages that I was getting from textbooks. Not only the message, but who was delivering the messages and the content. I began self-reflecting on the lessons that I was learning and about the people who were not learning these same lessons. Soon, I began to feel that education was just another form of segregation. Segregating those who are privileged enough or driven enough to make attending school a reality was the lens I started to use to see myself as an individual who was using education to better myself and my future. It was this thought process that led me to focus on the various spaces in education that played a part in the exclusionary nature of a group of people.

Meeting Black Student Quota

Getting an education is like getting the keys to a new car. You have all the tools and things you need to take you where you need to go. And, just like when you get a new car, you do not always have a place to go or know how to get there. However, imagine the people who never have gotten a new car or cannot even fathom what that feeling must be like. If you never experience something, how can you know how great it is? For anyone who has completed any level of education after high school, they know the feeling of graduating. Experiencing that liberation and sense of success can be the difference in someone sacrificing and making the decision to get an education, or deciding that attending school is not a choice that can add any value to their lives.

Depending on who you ask, some people believe that every single person has opportunities in life to succeed at whatever they want. No matter what their circumstances or experiences, some individuals believe that there are opportunities for everyone. If this was actually true, why do schools have to meet racial quotas for admissions? If everyone has the same opportunities there should not be anything in place to make sure blacks are represented. The reality is, people are not given the same opportunities. Being a black student means that you are entering a situation with negativity. If you are a black student who is articulate, smart, and show promise you are considered a better option; however, you still have the one strike of being black against you. Why does this matter? Let's say there are 11 spots open for students to enter a Master's program at a university. For those 11 spots, you have 11 whites, 4 Hispanics, 4 Blacks, 6 Asians and 3 others (I use "other" because some people identify this way). All these individuals hope to be accepted into this program. It is possible that this program could not have one single white person admitted. But let's be realistic; there will be the same amount of white people or more white people than all other races combined. No matter who is more qualified, we have to consider what their past experiences have been. It cannot be denied that when it comes to education, white people are given special treatment.

Over the past 10 years, there has been a stronger push for Historically Black Colleges/Universities or HBCUs to be considered as regular universities. The purpose of HBCUs was to educate black people. The fact that a different university had to be established to make sure black people could get an education is a problem in and of itself. Should this go to show how excluded black people are when it comes to education? Secondly, why do we have to identify a school as HBCU to begin with? Why don't we identify any others as predominantly race based schools? This is just another way black people are isolated and identified as "different."

Black History a Part of American History

Another issue black people face when it comes to education is what is taught to us. Learning about various wars, different historical landmarks, and historical events is important. However, what is also important is allowing the students to learn something about their heritages. This includes where they came from and who they are—not only for black children; children of other races should also receive this kind of cultural education. History is not just about how America won their wars and the tactics they used to do so. It is also about discovering America, who controlled the land first, how/when whites came to America, how the Indians had their land taken from them, norms that were institutionalized/colonized by whites, why slaves were brought over, what happened to the slaves when they were brought over, slaves who fought for freedom, how long it took for slaves to be free, and who owned slaves. Additionally, those who did not want the slaves to be free, individuals who were inspirational black leaders and what they did for slavery, the Civil Rights War and everything that happened because of it should be taught and respected. What has been increasingly missing from history books in school ranges from how blacks were treated, to how the north, south, east, and west treated blacks and other people of color, and the rights that blacks did not have even after slavery was abolished. In relation to these historical components, how our prison systems were established and how they have impacted the ways in which we continue to racialize people in our communities needs to be mentioned as well. The influence that various presidents have had on our country, the role they have each played in shaping history, and how slavery was established and abolished need to be presented for our children to better understand the foundation on which our country was built. Because this information is not discussed as a part of history, children grow up assuming a lot of things and not realizing they truly do not know. Unless you take additional time to learn about all of American history, there is no way to really know what is happening without being given the opportunities to gain this knowledge.

So the question that has to be asked is: "Why are we not talking about black history in our school systems?" This is a part of history! However, if you think about it, black history is the "ugly" part of American history. That outlines the greed, selfishness, isolation, mistreatment of an entire race, and the entitlement that still happens. But if it is not taught in detail people are not aware of the behavior or the extent of the behavior. Therefore, they do not have to understand the perspective of black people or begin to try and understand why blacks, then and now, continue to feel like they are not treated as equals. Have things gotten better? Yes. Are they better to the point that we, as black people, get treated fairly? Absolutely, not!

Institutional Racism and the Dominant Culture

During my Master's program, I first saw the terms "institutional racism" and "dominant culture" in a textbook. Interestingly, the terms actually appeared in an organizational textbook that was talking about why change could be hard for people and how to work around that change. That moment was when I realized these two terms played a big role in our educational systems, and they are the reason why various races are treated differently and why it is harder for minorities to overcome their skin color.

First let's look at Institutional Racism (IR) and understand how black people are on the shorter end of the stick when it comes to education. IR can be referred to specific groups targeted or isolated based on race. For education, this comes from the laws that are created that do not take into account how black children's lives are different and how they face different challenges. One of the first places you look to identify IR is to identify the policy makers, and who sits at the table when decisions need to be made. If the Board of Education does not have equal representation from the various types of students they are trying to impact, how can we expect these groups to help all children equally? For example, there should be people from all the school district's different races at these meetings. When rules are discussed, there should be at least a few people who can stand up for the children who come from low-income communities. Speaking to their experiences would give voice to their unheard voices. If this does not happen, it lays the foundation for those kids to be forgotten about. Once they are forgotten, any rules that come into play can be the reason why these kids lose out on being as educated equally with their racial counterparts. IR starts at the top, such as the policy makers and anyone who has any power to dictate what happens in our school systems. Running parallel to our decision makers is the allocation of teachers. If teachers who have a lot of accolades are sent to schools with a higher socioeconomic status, how does that serve our students who need a little bit more help learning? I am not suggesting that all of the best teachers should be sent to lower-income schools. But I am saying there should be a 50/50 split. Perhaps we should divide teachers in a way that is fair to all school districts. They could be given incentives to help these lower-income schools, instead of just allowing these schools to not flourish to their full potential. The allocation of teachers is something else the policy makers control, and whether they realize it or not, they can play a tremendous role in helping students get educated.

In addition, testing, whether it is standardized testing, or having children tested for disorders, are two other ways that IR impacts black children. Standardized testing was first put in place to measure intelligence and determine whether children had learned enough to proceed to the next grade. However, the problem with standardized tests is that a lot of people believe the tests indicate more of environmental and cultural differences. Secondly, getting tested for disorders is another roadblock for blacks. Due to the processes that are in place, the ways in which students are diagnosed for a disorder are hard, time consuming, and expensive. The rules label the child as having a disability, and this process is regulated by the policy makers as well. What this means is that there are procedures set to trickle-down to the students and their families, as they struggle to get children diagnosed. Essentially, taking part in these procedures allows for my children to be behind in their education and they may not learn as much as other students in their classes. Arguably, this then creates a cycle of children not being at the same educational level as other students, and for many, this will cause them to continually lag behind in their education.

One of the main reasons why IR exists is because of the dominant culture that has long existed in education. The dominant culture is the most influential and powerful social and political culture. It is the culture that we revert to when deciding what is deemed normal. This includes inclusive language, social views, religion, values, and decisions. Additionally, the reason this plays a role in education is because the dominant culture is white. So what white people do, how they learn information, and the experiences they have are often the basis of how we learn things. For example, I remember being in school and taking a test. One of the questions began with: "On a farm…" Students who have lived on a farm have some context of what a farm looks like, and they have an advantage reading this question. It might seem like a small thing, but if you hear the word "farm" and nothing comes to mind, how hard would that be to understand how you should interpret that information? However, those within the dominant culture are likely to be more familiar with "farm language" and have some type of context. The dominant culture also plays the biggest part in what children are taught. The example used previously in regard to being taught all of America's history, not just the things that make us sound great, illustrates how the dominant culture can dictate what is taught. Who do you think writes the history books? Who do you think identifies things that will be asked of students on their standardized testing? It is the dominant culture and everyone who is able to sit at the table to make these executive decisions.

IR and the dominant culture are elements that educators and policy makers should be consciously aware of because they are the ones who determine the type of education these students receive. Now the argument can be made that it is not a teacher's sole responsibility to educate a child. This can be true, as families do play a part in educating their children. But if you educate your child on one thing and they do not get this same type of education in school, this can cause more confusion in a child than anything else. As a child, my parents made me read black history books and books about people other than Harriet Tubman, Frederick Douglass, Martin Luther King Jr., and Malcolm X. At the time, it did not make sense why I had to do this because I heard a little bit about the others mentioned in school. Based on the limited knowledge I gained from these readings, I felt that I had a little bit of understanding about them. What I know now is that my parents were showing me that people other than those taught in school, were influential for black people. That was their way of educating me on more than I was being taught at school. They wanted me to understand more about my history, more than I would ever learn in school. Should schools only focus on black history? No. Should schools focus on all history equally and give the entire story about America? Yes. As much as black schools want to teach black students about black history, that same education should happen in white schools, and all schools that operate within the society controlled by the dominant culture. How else will we understand each other? And how else will we all get to know our history and understand the role it plays in our lives today? By keeping out, or monitoring the black history that is discussed in schools, we minimize and undermine the struggles blacks have had to endure. It also sends a subconscious message that black history is not important enough to share. Children are sponges at young ages and if they hear more back stories about people's trials and tribulations, that could make a significant impact on how they view black people moving forward. Why would we not want this to happen?

Lack of Publishing Perspective

Something else that happen in our school systems is the lack of diversity perspective in reading material. This might not seem like that big of a deal, because no matter who tells the story about history, it should be the same, right? Well, not exactly. For instance, think about a time you were sitting in a class/workshop and someone showed a picture of something. The way you initially looked at the picture was one way, but as the presenter talked about what they saw in the picture, you began to realize you did not see things their way. The same can be said if someone holds up a picture of a gun. Some people might tell one story while others might think it means something else. What makes a difference in how we tell the story is the lens through which we see the story and how that particular experience impacts you as an individual.

The same is true for people who write books. Take me, for example; I am writing this book from the perspective of a black woman, and it is influenced, or slanted, by my experiences. What I have seen and been through is different from other people, but I still have my own lens, and my lens is just as valid as anyone else's. Some of you might think I am absolutely crazy for the things I am writing about, but many of you can relate—if not to all of it, then probably the majority of the content. That begs the question—what about authors who write textbooks to educate the majority of us? Through what lens do they view the world? What perspective do they write from? If a black person authored a history book, what stories would they tell, and how would they differ from the ones selected by a white person writing the same history book? What about publishers? We all know certain publishers will only support a book if they think it will give them a particular kind of readership and a specific amount of money. For education, if we read books written from the viewpoints of people that we do not even relate to, how does that help educational growth? I have read thousands of books/articles from the time I started my Master's degree up until finishing my PhD. I can tell you within the first 5 pages of most things I read, I can determine the lens of the writer. How does this shape education and how is it discussed?

Having a diverse perspective can be the difference in a student not only understanding the story better, but understanding their neighbors, and others, in their communities better, as well. Education should bring us together and help to build strength together. In order for our nation to be successful, we have to understand and respect each other. We do not always have to agree on the same things, but we should at least be able to understand each other's perspectives. At the very least, we should be able to have some context as to why people have different feelings or thoughts about particular situations.

Questions:

1. What type of book would you write about with this picture?
2. What do you think the story is?
3. Would your story be the same as someone of a different race?

Conclusion

Being educated is about learning everything, not about being sheltered or only having certain information available. Education is power, and without that power, many people will not be able to reach their full potential. In America, we must do a better job of educating people about what has happened in the past, and what is really happening in the present. It should no longer be acceptable to isolate certain groups of people and not educate them at the same level. For some reason as a society, we are alright with having schools like Harvard, Stanford, and Yale. However, what do the graduates from those universities learn about black history? If they are indeed being groomed to be our leaders, then how can they understand anything about the people they are going to be employing and working with if they do not know anything about them or their history? Lastly, how do these schools help us as a society? Yes, they might help the people who are admitted to them excel in life, but what about the people who cannot afford it, or are deemed not smart enough to attend one of those schools? Does it help America to not give those students the education and the advantages of the students that attend these prestigious schools? Perhaps the real question should be: Who benefits from this separation of education and who suffers the most from it?

Education helps one case cease being intimidated by strange situations.

~ Maya Angelou

Six

ORGANIZATIONS

...for which it stands

O rganizations are often thought about as places that are fair, consistent, and allow everyone a chance to be successful. However, just like in other environments, there are inequities that happen in the workplace. Our country has put things into place to try to ensure that everyone is given a fair chance. But the reality is black people are still on the receiving end of some unfair treatment. Let's start with the obvious, such as Affirmative Action. For those of you who do not know, Affirmative Action is an act that permits companies to agree to not discriminate against minorities. Once again, the simple fact that this has to be put in play to make sure minorities are not discriminated against already proves my point. Why would you have to have this law if everything was fair and consistent? The simple answer is if Affirmative Action was not the law, millions of people would be discriminated against.

Affirmative Action might have been enacted to help minorities have opportunities, and be seen as equals from their employers. But, there are ways around Affirmative Action. For example, if there is a manager position available and a company has minorities interview for the job, that is enough to indicate that all the "boxes have been checked." As a black person, it is an insult to interview for a job when you know there is no way you will be chosen. Working in various industries and seeing black people get passed over for jobs they were more qualified for in favor of someone else is frustrating. It also raises the question: How can black people get the promotions and the higher jobs they seek if the color of their skin is constantly part of the decision making process? Throughout this section, different roadblocks for black people will be highlighted. In organizations, there is a lack of opportunities for blacks. Even with Affirmative Action in place, organizations still find some not-so-discreet ways to keep black people isolated.

"Culture Fit"

For about the last 10 years, the term "culture fit" has appeared for managers to fill out about potential applicants. At first glance, reading "culture fit" and figuring out why it is necessary seems obvious. The word "culture" refers to the environment the candidate will be working in. The word "fit" is how that person *fits* within that culture. Sounds easy enough, right? The problem is that *culture* is defined by the environment in an organization or by how the person's culture fits in with the current employees. For example, let's say you have a group of white, highly educated men on a team, and you interview a white man and black man who are both typically educated. From their resumes and initial phone screens, both men appear to be a great fit, perhaps with the black man even being a closer match to the company's needs. However, on interview day, both men show up, both do their interviews, and the white candidate is ultimately offered the job. Would you like to speculate on the reason for the black man not getting the job? You guessed it. He was not a "culture fit." Now the question has to be asked: Why was he not a culture fit? What did he do that gave him a strike? This is a real example of something that happened right in front of my eyes. While it was happening, I could not help but go online and research the words "culture fit," just to see how the decision was being made. Not one time during the discussion did anyone give me a specific reason as to how the black man was not a culture fit. What specifically did he do during the interview that caused him to no longer be the top choice for the position?

Culture fit has become a way that organizations can get around the Affirmative Action law. By saying someone is not a culture fit, job candidates can be excluded from being considered for a job, and because this is a relatively new term, organizations do not have to identify the specifics as to *how* someone is *not* a culture fit. This is happening because the reality in the United States is, during interviews there are certain questions that cannot be asked. Unless the candidate freely volunteers information, there are things that organizations might not know about them. So to exclude someone based on culture fit when you do not know personal things about the candidate is unfair. In saying this, we all know sometimes you can tell certain things based on how someone answers a question or by the examples they give. In addition, they might not be in line for what you are looking for. If that is the case, the reason for not moving forward with the hiring process is not a culture fit.

By definition, culture fit is the probability that a candidate will be able to conform and adapt to the core values and collective behaviors that make up an organization. The words that stand out to me in this sentence are *conform* and *collective behaviors*. These two words are important because black people get stereotyped for being confrontational, aggressive, ignorant, and uneducated. If we are all of those things, how could we possibly conform to an organization's values, or even more so, how can our collective behaviors be in line with what an organization wants? Obviously, that representation of black people is not accurate, but that is what the media shows constantly. The truth is, this is how a lot of people see black people, which limits us in a lot of ways, especially in organizations.

Being Black in Organizations

Being employed by a company does not mean that being black goes away. This sounds a little bit daunting, but the truth is getting a job is just the beginning of challenges that black people face. Stop and think about the company you work for. How many black leaders, male or female, do you see in your organization? Now obviously all organizations are structured differently, but there are generally leaders, managers, directors, etc., in every organization. This means there are ample opportunities to have diverse leaders. Generally, there are more leaders in organizations who are black, as opposed to them being managers and directors. When you think about this on a larger scale, who does this put at the table when policies are developed or key decisions are made in organizations?

Another issue for black people, that happens frequently in organizations is the need to "be aware of our blackness." What exactly does this mean? Unfortunately, the perception of black people is not always favorable, and the one that can have the most negative impact in an organization, is a black person being aggressive. Because of this perceived aggressiveness, we have to be careful with the tone of voice we use, our facial expressions, body language, how we express ourselves, and how we have conversations. Why is this? Why should an individual have to monitor themselves in such great detail? Naturally, different ideas and conversations will bring up different emotions in people. But when you are black, you have to make sure when these differences emerge, the reaction does not come off too harshly. What usually ends up happening is that if a black person does speak up it comes off harsh and too direct. Unfortunately, more often than not, black people will sit in a meeting and think about how they are going to say something. However, the way it sounds in their head may be different than the way it sounds out loud. Often, many blacks sit in the meeting in silence. This is happening at your organizations right now, I can almost guarantee it.

Diversity Committees

In almost every organization, there is a diversity committee that is put in place to make sure everyone in the organization is treated fairly regardless of their differences. However, just because someone is black does not mean they want to be a part of the diversity committee. We all understand the reason behind diversity being important and why organizations spend time and money making sure everyone is comfortable. The reality of diversity committees is that organizations usually do not have a clear vision or purpose for the committee. Yes, there are catchy missions and conversations about what the committee means to the organization, but what exactly is the purpose? Is it to bring awareness to people about diversity? Is it to bring a bunch of different people together to have conversations? Is it to make minorities feel comfortable? What is the purpose? The better question is: How are companies monitoring the success of these committees?

All of these questions are important because these committees are in place in almost any organization you can think of. However, if the problems of not having any black leaders is not addressed, and if black people are silenced based on not wanting to be judged for the things they do say in meetings, how can these committees be successful? The point of a diversity committee is to be supportive of the diversity in an organization and to find ways to avoid making minorities feel isolated. Too many times these committees are not focused on the main issue, and they fail to have real conversations with people. The truth is, some people are not comfortable around certain people, and sometimes a race is excluded from a conversation before a decision is made. All cultures might not have been in consideration before something has happened in an organization. All of these things should be addressed in diversity committees. Pay attention to diversity committees in your organization. Are they helping move the needle on diversity issues? Is the committee listening to issues and solving them efficiently? These are all questions where the answer should be yes. If the answer is no, imagine how hard it would be for a black person to be open and honest within a committee when they do not have full confidence that real issues can be solved?

Black Events
One thing that happens a lot in organizations is black people being put in odd situations at work because of real life events. When a teen gets shot or something bad happens in the black community, the thoughts

and feelings that people have about these experiences do not stop when they arrive at work. Due to this, it can create an unsettling environment for everyone within the organization. During these times, it is important that the comments people make are not insensitive or demeaning. When the verdict of Trayvon Martin was delivered, I remember hearing whispers from people at work and individuals giving their two cents on the matter. What they did not realize was that for a lot of people that case raised a lot of fear, anger, and distrust in our criminal justice system. It also raised questions about how black lives were treated and if black people were important. This might sound crazy to someone who does not understand how going through this situation can impact someone's life.

Sensitivity has to be a part of the work place, because without it employees do not feel comfortable in their work environments. By no means will people all respond to things the same way, and that is normal. What does need to happen is people need to be aware of everyone in their organization and how these events can translate to people having some discomfort? For black people, it is important that we have a safe place to be able to deal with events that are happening and not feel like we have to be silenced because of our view on the topic. Not everyone will understand the magnitude of every situation, but that does not make it right to be rude or disrespectful to the people who are impacted by these unjust events.

Conclusion

Understanding how black people feel in organizations can help to create a better environment for black employees. As well, having conversations around how these negative thoughts and feelings can be changed. It is important for black people to feel included in organizations, not because affirmative action says they have to be included, but because organizations see the importance of having them be engaged. Let me acknowledge the fact that black people are not the only people who are working in organizations, but that there are black people working in organizations and getting their buy in and creating an environment where we can actively and honestly be a part of conversations. Silencing a group of people cannot positively help an organization reach goals. People of other races might come into an organization with a preconceived notion about blacks. It is up to the organization to make sure collectively their employees are treating everyone with respect.

Change will not come if we wait for some other person or some other time. We are the ones we've been waiting for. We are the change that we seek.

~ President Barack Obama

Seven

Entertainment

...one nation

G rowing up in the 90s, TV was completely different than it is now when it comes to representing black people. For starters, there were shows like *The Fresh Prince of Bel Air, Family Matters,* and *The Cosby Show*. These shows had rich black families who addressed real black issues. Shows like this not only helped as talking points for black families, but they also helped a lot of blacks set goals. Similarly, people in society got an inside look at black families being successful and mild-mannered, which opens the eyes of society to a different view of blacks. *A Different World* was another black show that focused on black students at a historically black university. This show was another positive reflection of black students being in college, achieving goals, having fun, and growing as individuals. Adult shows like *Martin* and *Living Single* were not only funny, but reflective of how black adults, single, friends, married, and families deal with real-life situations. Each of these 6 shows focused on black people and their overall life experiences. Part of what television provides is an example for people to aspire to be, as well as a way for people to see experiences they would not normally see.

Becoming familiar and comfortable with a culture or a race that is different from yours is not an easy task. However, having things like television shows highlight experiences from different cultures plays a big part in people becoming engaged in understanding something that is different. However, the problem starts when television shows no longer show positive outlooks on a particular race. Believe it or not, people internalize what they see. This is not only an issue of the negative images and storylines of black people, but there is also a need to show the struggle black people endure in the real world.

White-Dominant Shows

There are several shows that have had a long running tenure, but there have not been black people in lead roles on these shows. Let's take the *Bachelor/Bachelorette* series. *The Bachelor* has been on TV since 2002 and *The Bachelorette* has been on since 2012. However, there has never been a black bachelor or bachelorette. Why not? Does ABC not think black people would like to find love? What is the issue with having a black bachelor or bachelorette? Who would it hurt? Next, on each series, there is never more than one or two black contestants on the show. Why? Lastly, what message does this really send? Are black people not worthy of being loved? Are they not pretty enough or important enough to carry a show? These are the types of internal questions that not only black people begin to ask, but also cause white people to think the same thing. We do not have to collectively agree that this is happening, but when you think about it, how can it not be happening? Let's be honest. Why hasn't there been a black bachelor or bachelorette on the show?

Taking this even further, why don't more shows have more leading black people in roles, or why are there not more black people on the show to begin with. There are so many examples of this, but only a few that will be discussed. For entertainment shows that have judges like *American Idol, The Voice,* and *The X Factor,* there is usually one black person in the role of a judge on the show. If you look at the entertainment industry, there are a many black people who have had success. Where are these black people when it comes to television shows? Each of these shows generally rotate the black person. Once one black person leaves, they replace that black person with another. However, looking at the entire panel, more times than not there are more white people on the panel than any other race. Now, by no means should every seat on every show be filled by a black person, but the real question is why does it always have to be dominated by white people? What would be the harm in having two black judges on *The Voice*? Obviously, *American Idol* is over, but the questions still remain. Why are there not more black people on the judge panel? Why, as a society, do we have to make sure there are more white people than black people on the show? Or, really any minority? So many people watch these shows and with a black presence, you must consider that with the contestants, is this the message these shows want to be sending about race and power?

If you think about the shows you have watched over the past 10 years, how many shows have shown black people in a positive light? How many of those shows have black people as main actors/actress? How many shows have black people being successful in what they do? These are important questions to ask yourself because if the answer is a low number that shows you how black people are portrayed on television, or that they do not have a presence in leading roles. It is unfortunate, with TV being so influential, it can impact how people see an entire race of people, but it is happening.

Reality TV

I think reality TV has completely discredited and created new roadblocks for black people. Shows like *Love and Hip Hop* (including spinoffs), *Basketball Wives, Married to Medicine, The Bad Girls Club*, and what is worse, *The Real Housewives of Atlanta*, have black people acting ignorant, aggressive, irresponsible, insensitive, and classless just to use a few adjectives. For the shows that have men on them, the men are usually not faithful, liars, and show zero compassion toward the women they are hurting. How does this uplift black people and how does this help shed a positive light on blacks? These shows align themselves with stereotypes that society places on black people. Why is this happening? Let's think about who is in charge of the narrative. Yes, some of these shows have black producers and some of the producers play a big part in how the show plays out. The bigger picture is that the networks make more money on viewership and advertising, and it does not matter to them if the product they put out misrepresents and poorly labels an entire race. As long as it makes money, nothing else matters. Now, are there white reality shows that degrade white men and women? Maybe, but how many of those shows are on air?

As a whole, these black shows create an image and a narrative about black people that is not accurate. For someone who has not been raised around a lot of black people, who may have nothing more to go on than these shows, these ridiculous stories may be seen as realities. These shows do not teach kids about the importance of having goals, setting priorities, and becoming functional members of society. Instead, they show these people spending money, "looking good," not being faithful to their spouses, destroying relationships, and defending themselves! Why aren't there white shows like this? Because white people act like this too? Instead, white people get the more "real housewives," and we see their fancy houses, rich friends, and upscale lifestyles. The reality is that I know more white people who do not live like that than I know who do. Some of you are thinking, *Wait what about the real housewives of Atlanta or Potomac?* They have black people. True, they do. However, on the Atlanta housewives show, there are usually some type of physical altercations that happen, which feeds into the negative narrative of stereotyping black people. As far as Potomac…. the jury is still out.

Looking at the reality shows that are on TV now, this is a reflection of the stereotypes of blacks. There are several shows that depict black people in a negative light, which causes people to internalize what they think of black people. The reality is that the majority of black people are not like what is shown on outlandish shows. No matter how much money the people in these shows make, why are there always blacks getting into physical altercations, saying loud and degrading things about each other, and not acting civilized? This is extremely sad and does not do a great job of showing how black people actually live.

Movies

In 2016, the #Oscarssowhite hashtag reappeared. When things like this happen, looking on social media and going through news feeds is always interesting because people's opinions are always all over the place. However, the majority of black people have similar thoughts. Why were there not any black people nominated for awards? Why don't black people get the same movie opportunities as white people? Each of these questions are very familiar and continue to need to be asked. The truth is that we are not just asking this question for movie roles, but we are asking these questions about jobs, education, and our justice system as well. This is about opportunity, and offering the same opportunities to people of all races.

One interesting thing is that when a movie is made about black people and slavery, that movie wins awards. For example, *12 Years a Slave* and *Django Unchained* were movies that revolved around slavery and how black people were treated. However, the people who win the big awards are the white people who were in the movie. Lupita Nyong'o won for best supporting actor for *12 Years a Slave*. But, this was still for being in a supporting role, not for being the lead actress. For *The Help,* which was another movie where black women who were essentially slaves were being interviewed, Octavia Spencer, who is a black woman, won for a supporting actress role. It seems as though black people are good enough to make a movie about and good enough to win supporting awards, but not quite good enough to take home awards for lead actor/actresses roles. Sidney Poitier, Denzel Washington, Jamie Foxx, Forest Whitaker are the only male black actors who have won Oscars for best actor. However, Halle Berry is the only black woman who has ever won an Oscar for best actress.

First, many people will comment on the other awards that black actors and actresses have won. But we all know the Oscars are considered the highest awards for actors and actresses, so the other awards that have been reviewed are great, but remember this is about the opportunity. Secondly, why do black people have to settle for not getting a highly coveted award? Just like artists, an MTV video award is great, but getting a Grammy is the accomplishment that everyone wants. The real question is why don't black people get the opportunities that whites get when it comes to film? The real answer is that we will never know. Just think about how many times, Leonardo Dicaprio, Tom Hanks, Jack Nicholson, Matt Damon, Matthew Mcconaughey, Brad Pitt, and Johnny Depp have been nominated for an Oscar. I can almost promise you just those actors alone have double the amount of wins over all the black male and female actors and actresses combined. If this does not speak to opportunity, I am not sure what will.

Music Industry

A familiar place where black people are more often criticized than whites is in the music industry. Black rappers often get criticized for the things that rap is about and the lyrics they use. People formulate opinions about how the artists (blacks) must be based on these lyrics. However, if you look at white artists they do not experience this same treatment. MackLemore and Eminem are two artists who come to mind when considering white artists who are free to rap about their struggles and the things they see, and people love it. They are always praised for how well-rounded they are and what good rappers they are. They rap about the same things black artists rap about, their experiences. Often, many of the rappers come from low-income neighborhoods and experience a lot of painful situations. These situations are what they rap about. Whether it is the unfair treatment they get from police, women, cars, money, etc., these are things the majority of rappers deal with. Do some of them fabricate? Of course. Just like when Eminem raps, he degrades celebrities and makes up stories; other artists are no different. There is some truth, and false statements in raps, but that is to be expected. The bigger issue is why white rappers get more credit for their raps and less backlash than black rappers?

Similarly, Kendrick Lamar is an artist who writes music to talk about his struggle and the things he has seen throughout his life. Being from Compton, California, he has experienced a lot of things that many of us would never even imagine. However, it is through these experiences that he is able to speak his truths and put out music that is reflective of what he has gone through. For him, his music is a way for some people to understand what they themselves continue to go through and it is relatable. Kendrick Lamar performed an amazing reflective piece at the Grammy's. His performance encompassed the experiences of black people and others who are aware of the black struggles he identified with. It was art and depicted many struggles that black people endure. His music is very real and extremely authentic, but because Kendrick Lamar is black, people do not listen to his message as intently. Then there is MackLemore, who has written now two songs titled White Privilege 1 and White Privilege 2. Both of the songs are honest and reflective of how white privilege works and the perks that white people have in society. Since MackLemore is white, I guess that gives him the green light to acknowledge that white privilege exists and people are more comfortable hearing it from him. Black artists sing about the same thing, but for the majority of listeners, the message gets lost.

At one point Lady Gaga and Nicki Minaj were both wearing outlandish outfits on the red carpet, during performances, and at a variety of other public appearances. However, Lady Gaga was accepted for wearing these things, and the media always waited to see what she was wearing so they could talk about as "artistry." On the other hand, Nicki Minaj wore similarly outlandish outfits and she received labels of not being as respectable as Lady Gaga. Why? What is the difference between these two women? They are both artists, both seeking attention, and both expressing themselves in their own ways. But, one person was labeled for doing things that were perceived differently, and the other was simply idolized for being different. It is obvious which person received which label. At the present time, neither of these artists continues to wear these outlandish outfits and are both widely successful women. So clearly, their reasons behind what they wore worked out in their favor.

When you look at the music industry as a whole, the great thing about it is that it allows people to express themselves any way they see fit. Unfortunately, much like other things in America, black people have to deal with a different set of rules than white artists. We can act like it is the same, but the truth is if a black artist and white artist sing about the same things, the black person will be deemed as the one complaining and the white artist will be seen as speaking facts. One of the things about music that makes it so diverse is the ability for people to be able to tell their stories and articulate how different events of their lives dictate how they get through things. In essence, a lot of these life events shape how and what these artists talk about, and that is what makes music so great. Everyone is different, and the way one person tells a story based on someone else's experiences, is how we can determine who we like and who we do not like. This should be respected, whether the artist is white or black. That is the perception we need to change as fans of music. A white person should not get more or less credit than a black person who may be performing the same lyrics.

Conclusion

Entertainment could have a tremendous impact on how people perceive black people and can set the tone of their expectations. It is unfortunate that black people are portrayed negatively in the media, whether on TV shows, reality shows, movies, or in music. By no means should television be focused on the messages they are presenting to viewers because they are doing it for the money. However, as viewers, we should take responsibility in the things and events we see, and more importantly, become more aware of the ways in which black people are unfairly being negatively portrayed. In addition, as viewers, the conclusions we come to should be based on truths about people, rather than solely formulating thoughts and opinions based on inaccurate portrayals.

I had crossed the line. I was free; but there was no one to welcome me to the land of freedom. I was a stranger in a strange land.

~ Harriet Tubman

Eight

The System

...under God

If there is one part of our society that is the most unfair, biased, judgmental, and perplexing, it is our criminal justice system. The most consistent belief that exists is that people who are low on funds do not stand a chance. The obvious reason is because they are not able to afford great lawyers, resources, and experts. Some of them are not educated about the positions they are in and how to change them. After all, someone has to be placed in jails and pay fines to keep our jail systems up and running. Our prison systems are supposed to be a place for rehabilitation. But they have become a place that just houses people as a way to make profit. Additionally, not having enough funding for these people puts less attention on rehabilitation. The recidivism rate of people going back to prison after they have been released is almost half.

In July 2015, a report identified America as the country that incarcerates people at the highest rate. According to the *Federal Bureau of Prisons*, there are 207,847 people incarcerated in federal prisons. Roughly half (48.6%) are in for drug offenses. According to the Bureau of Justice Statistics, there are 1,358,875 people in *state prisons*. Of these, 16% have a drug crime as their most serious offense. There were also 744,600 inmates in county and city jails. Just to clarify, drug crimes are often considered to be nonviolent crimes because they do not always involve the use of force or cause injury to another person. Nonviolent crimes are often measured by economic damage or loss to the victim. Looking at these statistics, think about how many people are displaced from their families. Also, why are people serving so many years for nonviolent crimes and drug offenses? How are we growing and developing as a country if we fill prisons up more and more with people who commit nonviolent crimes? The question has to be asked, what are the benefits of giving people long sentences?

Levels in the Criminal Justice System

There are so many levels to our criminal justice system, and unfortunately, these layers are what creates the limitation for the people they are trying to prosecute. It makes sense to start with the lowest level in this chain and work our way up.

SUSPECTS

If someone asked you to identify the first image that popped in your head when someone says "criminal," what image appears? This question is asked because if people can close their eyes and have any type of image appear, that means as a society there is a perception of what we perceive as good versus what we perceive as bad. This is a problem because cops are people too. If we think this, why would a cop think differently? The reality is a criminal does not have a standard look and there are no specific ways to identify a criminal. However, if you take a look at people who get labeled as criminals, there seems to be a trend. Black people are not given any leniency when it comes to being perceived as criminals. If a black person is in a neighborhood that it does not look like we belong to, or if we are driving a car that looks too expensive, we look suspicious. However, if we do make eye contact, or if we are loud, quiet, too calm, or with a bunch of other black people, we always look suspicious. This might sound outrageous or overly exaggerated, but it is the truth. Black people are guilty of being black, and because of that, we are more vulnerable to being harassed by police officers.

Do other races commit crimes? Absolutely, but for some reason when your skin is black you are seen as a bigger threat. There are not any actual statistics that depict black people as ones who are involved in more crimes than white people. In addition, black people are not a part of any massive terrorist groups, and there are no wars against black people that anyone wants to admit to. So the even bigger question is why is this happening? Why are black people so easily identified as suspects? This question could be asked 100 times to various different groups of people, and there may be several answers going around. But the only answer that consistently will appear is race. We are all human beings and sometimes the only thing that separates us, that is easily detected, is race.

Cops

Where do I even begin? Let me start off by saying being a cop cannot be an easy job. Dealing with criminals on a daily basis, trying to decipher between the good, the bad, the right, and the wrong cannot be easy. Not to mention—you are a target because the police vehicle is easily identifiable. Additionally, some people just do not like authority, which means cops have to face battles and disgruntled people in difficult situations often. Nonetheless, knowing all that comes with the job, and knowing the oath that is taken to protect and serve, it is inexcusable to target a group of people based on the fact that they are vulnerable. We can say it is not because they are less privileged, since the neighborhoods that are constantly targeted by the police are considered a threat and people are constantly getting pulled over. The people who are more often than not victims of police brutality are often people in these neighborhoods, and it happens to a group that police officers have deemed less privileged. No, all cops are not bad; and no, all police squads do not go into their jobs determined to pick on black people. However, many do! The fact that police officers act like this is not a fact is a problem in and of itself. In every single job, there are bad seeds. But for some reason, it is hard for people to understand that there can be bad cops! Just like there are priests who unfortunately abuse children. For whatever reason, people take a turn and become something that nobody expected. So this notion that only a criminal can go from being a law abiding citizen to a criminal, but a cop cannot go from a good cop to a bad cop is crazy.

Cops are the most organized legal gang that we have on this planet. They are not only structured well, but they have authority and support from a lot of people just because they are cops. The job of a cop is to keep our neighborhoods safe, not to become a figure that a group of people try to avoid out of the fear that they will become a victim of circumstance. Again, not all cops are bad and not all cops are a part of the gang. I strongly believe there are more good cops than bad cops. However, the bad cops are the ones who set the precedent for the good ones. When it comes to arresting and putting people into the system, this all begins with the cops. Because without them making an arrest there would not be suspects for prosecutors and judges to reprimand. We must consider carefully what this all means. We all know there has to be an incentive for cops to make these arrests, and for the suspects to be taken into custody. So, what is it?! Simple. Money!

When someone gets pulled over and gets a ticket, the money that is paid towards that ticket goes to that particular precinct. When a cop makes an arrest and someone goes to jail, that puts that suspect in the system which:

1. allows them to get a fine
2. puts them in the criminal justice quicksand, which is hard to get out of once you are in—which equates to more money being paid out by the suspect.
3. and, the cops are able to maintain their quotas—which in turn validates their job and the hours they are getting paid for.

In essence, police officers are the start of the process that is the criminal justice system. Although their tactics are questionable, the biases and inequities do not stop with officers.

PROSECUTORS

Once these suspects are brought in and booked, the prosecutors determine what happens next, and they are all about winning cases. For them, winning a case can be getting a plea deal signed or prevailing at trial. If cops are the ranking council part of the "gang," then prosecutors are essentially the leader of the gang. They get to make the final decisions on what will happen to each of the suspects' cases. If the case is strong enough, what evidence is needed and what angle they need to take for the case becomes a process. That being said, they basically have all the power in decision making. Prosecutors and cops are essentially partners in crime, no pun intended. Since they are responsible for bringing cases to trial and getting a conviction, they get to decide if a case has enough evidence to be brought to trial.

With all the recent cases of white cops killing black people, it has been the prosecutors who decided not to bring these cases to trial. Even worse is when they have grand juries, and they are the ones that decided what evidence was presented or not presented. The real issue with this is when the person who should be brought to trial is a cop, or someone they work closely with. How can they actually present a case that is strong? Nobody really knows if they do, but the fact that this question has to be asked points to a bigger issue. How much do prosecutors push for justice to be served when that justice could land an ally in jail? What happens when the victim is black? The prosecutors did not even want to bring Trayvon Martin's case to the grand jury, and later, it was the media attention that was the deciding factor. These prosecutors want to make sure they protect their own versus the people they are supposed to be serving and protecting.

JUDGES

Although the judges are not on the front line of making decisions, they are still an important piece of the puzzle. Judges ultimately sign off on sentences and determine bail. This might not seem like a big deal, but these two pieces are extremely important factors in the injustices that black people get for their crimes. Here is how. At the beginning of the process when someone is arrested and they go see a judge, the judge determines bail based on a lot of factors. But, the main issues that need to be determined are: the ability to flee, and the severity of the crime. The consistency at which judges give black suspects larger bail is ridiculous. For example, Dylann Roof's bond, the white male who is suspected of shooting a bunch of black people to death in a black church in South Carolina was given one million dollars' bail. Tremaine Wilbourn, who was suspected of killing a white cop, was given 10 million dollars' bail. Allen Bullock, a Baltimore teen who was arrested for damaging a police car window during the Freddie Gray protest, was given a $500,000 bail. However, the cops who were accused of killing Freddie Gray were given bail ranging from $250,000 - $350,000 bail. This list could go on. But the point is that it is happening. What is worse about this process is, as mentioned before, these defendants cannot always afford good defense lawyers, or even lawyers who have time to catch up on a case. So when judges make their decisions, they see who is representing the defendants and the prosecution has given the judge all the information they can to determine why they should stay behind bars. These judges know what they are doing. We can act like black people are not getting higher bails than white people, but that is just not the case. Take some time to research what is happening in our systems because what is happening is not balanced or fair.

Secondly, judges determine sentences for defendants. For some reason, crimes that involve drugs give people higher sentences than the crimes that damage people's lives like rape, money fraud, and sometimes even murder (depending on who is murdered). It does not take a rocket scientist to determine which race is more likely to commit what type of crimes. The interesting part about this is that some people say there are just as many white people selling or involved with drugs as there are black people. But it is the black people who are caught at higher rates. Either way, how is a person who rapes a child and strips away someone's innocence less of a criminal than a drug dealer? Drug dealers are not forcing people to buy drugs. That is a choice that people make own their own, but they are punished more harshly. We have people who have stolen millions and millions of dollars from the elderly, sick, and hardworking individuals, yet they get shorter sentences than drug dealers. Why?

A defendant cannot adequately defend themselves if they do not have the funds. Our system is set up in a way that makes sure if you do not have any money, you just become another number in the system. At the end of the day, the people sitting in our jails are there because they are waiting…for trials, sentencing, or serving time. They have become a number. A number in a criminal justice system can make a profit, and more often than not, the profits come from the misfortune and bad decisions of others. The idea of prisons being a place people can be rehabilitated is no longer true because now companies can make millions. Some of them make billions by keeping prisons full. The question remains: Who wins in this scenario and who loses? This is a cycle and is happening in all of our cities and states to more and more black people.

Getting Tangled

There are steps set in place that are supposed to help people who are suspects in crimes, but they are not that helpful in the long run. Consider, if you will, bail bondsmen. There are companies that put up the bail bond to get people released while they await trial. Of course, there is a catch because this costs money. If someone does not have the means to use this avenue, then it is not helpful. On the other end, if someone does have the money to get out on bail, and they agree to pay the money, they are still responsible to pay back the money in the original agreement. For example, if someone's bail was set at $150,000, a bail bondsman could get that client out on bail for 10% payment or $15,000. Once released, the client would be responsible for showing up to all the events that have to deal with their trial because they have an obligation to the courts. If the person had the $15,000 to give to the bail bondsman upfront, great. But if not, in order to pay the bail, people arrange payment plans, give up titles to their houses, and often do whatever it takes in order to pay bail. This is important because not everyone can pay to be released from jail, and even more, these people are paying for their freedom. How is that true if the purpose of the court of law is to consider people "innocent until proven guilty?" Being a suspect can still cost you a ridiculous amount of money.

Think about the people who cannot afford to pay for this bail. What happens to them? Nothing. They sit in jail until their trial, and in turn, start losing their lives. How can someone sustain a job, family relationships, and maintain their own confidence if they are in jail for a crime they may or may not be guilty of? Another major hurdle for these suspects is getting an attorney who can actually help them build their cases to defend themselves in court. We all know about our "right to an attorney and if you cannot afford an attorney, one will be appointed to you." What this does not mention is the lack of attorneys who take cases and the extremely limited amount of time that these "free" lawyers can spend on these cases. Some people are sitting in jail and waiting for a free lawyer to be appointed.

Going through a bail bondsman, sitting in jail, awaiting trial, and getting an attorney who does not really have the time or resources to help is the standard for suspects. However, the frustrations and unfairness start way before this. In order to understand the inequities, it is important to see how many pieces there are to this equation.

Prisons

Private prisons often have occupancy limits they have to meet. Yes, that is making sure they are full enough so they are meeting their contractual agreements. Money is paid to prisons based on how many inmates they have, so the fewer inmates a prison has the less funding they get. These prisons charge the government; that is how they are maintained and make money. The prison population continues to go up.

Obviously, some prisons are at capacity and the fees to keep them locked up are not cheap for taxpayers. However, there are many states that have legalized contracting prison labor through private corporations. There are phones, food, cleaning supplies, security cameras, and various things inside the prison that have to be provided by companies. These companies set the rates for the prisons, and they collect their checks from the government as well. Prisons make these companies billions of dollars a year. It is important for these inmates to be in prison for as long as possible because the prisons get money from them being there. Additionally, so do these companies.

Why is this happening and what types of people are being impacted by the way things are functioning? Black people! Look at the population of people that are in prisons. Look at who is becoming just another inmate so money can be collected. Who is more expendable? Rich people do not have to deal with this cycle of becoming a number because they do not have to be in jail until they stand trial. But when you are not as fortunate, you could potentially lose your job, become a burden to your family, and have your life derailed—all for being a suspect to a crime, and not yet even convicted of a crime.

Still not convinced about how the system has the ability to ruin people's lives? Think about the people who leave prisons and the lives they return to. There is a multitude of limitations for felons waiting for them when they return to their environments. Felons cannot bear arms, obtain certain jobs, travel out of the country, vote, join the military, lease an apartment, get aid for school, or even become a tattoo artist. Of course different states have different rules for what you can and cannot do, but this is a list of the most common things. If you have limitations on jobs you can get and you have issues getting a place to live, what exactly are you supposed to do? Even getting funds to help out with school costs disappear, so how are you expected to create a better future for yourself and your family? This is why having rehabilitation or opportunities available for people that are in the system or getting out of the system is important.

Interrogations

Unfortunately, there are other aspects of the criminal justice system that also allow inequities to happen. Each of these topics play various roles in the process of the system, but they are all damaging and create advantages for police officers and the system. One thing to ask yourself is what type of people suffer the most with all of these things that happen to people every day.

LYING ABOUT EVIDENCE

During interrogation, cops use a tactic that allows them to lie about the actual evidence they have available. Some people might see this as something they should be allowed to do, but there are a few problems with this tactic. First, when someone is in an interrogation room, they are not in an environment they are used to, and because of that, there is a large amount of fear in this situation. We all can remember times when our parents or someone in authority started questioning our actions. Your heart starts beating faster, your palms start to sweat, and you start to question your own actions. People being interrogated by cops, go through these same stages, and unfortunately, it leads to suspects admitting to things they did not do.

Secondly, when some cops lie about evidence, they put the blame on someone the suspect loves and respects, leading them to want to take the blame for something they did not do. Merely placing the blame on a loved one can cause someone to start thinking about taking the blame for something they are not responsible. An example of this would be if the person being interrogated was a man and the detectives conducting the interview started to place the blame on his sister. A lot of men would take the blame for something if they felt like the evidence places their sister in the line of fire. This sets up these suspects to start accepting the lies they are being told. Once a suspect starts admitting to things they cannot take any of it back. What they admit to becomes a part of the evidence that will be used against them in court.

TIME SPENT INTERROGATING

Another part of interrogations that works in the favor of the system is the amount of time a suspect can be interrogated and the type of interrogation they receive. Holding a suspect for 5 hours and grilling them about their actions is not fair. If you are supposed to be innocent until proven guilty, how can you be grilled and treated like you are guilty for 5 hours? These detectives are trained for what they do, and if it takes them 5 hours—and in some cases longer—they need more training. Not only do they hold these suspects for long periods of time in a room, their tactics can be extremely aggressive and demeaning. They do not know if the person they are talking to has a mental illness, confidence issues, or what the other person is going through. These tactics are harmful. I am aware that some of you might be thinking, "Yeah, but these people are criminals so they deserve it." Everyone who gets treated like this is not a criminal. If there is straightforward evidence that leads these detectives to ask tough questions, I understand. But a lot of times, that is not the case. They fabricate information and try to get someone to take responsibility for whatever was done. In that instance, there is no reason to treat these people harshly. What if they did not do it? They are being yelled at and crucified only to later be released. This can be a life altering event—all for nothing.

Something else you might be thinking is, "Yeah, but these people can ask for a lawyer and not have to go through this." That is also correct. However, remember the question that was asked before starting this section: What types of people suffer from these tactics? The answer is uneducated, oppressed people. Instead of taking advantage of the fact that they do not know their rights, they should be treated as innocent people. That is what they are, right? Innocent until proven guilty. Also, remember there is a big difference in the way some people live compared to others. Some people have seen enough television, movies, or learned in school that when a cop is questioning you, you have the right to ask for an attorney and it will stop. However, people who are not as privileged, do not spend their time in front of a television. Think about how you feel when you are scared. Do you think logically and make the best decisions? The bigger question is, just like our system says, what happened to "innocent to proven guilty?"

Shooting to Kill

An issue that is back in the forefront is why do cops shoot to kill? Or more directly, why do they shoot innocent black men multiple times in the chest and head when they can do less damage with one or two shots below the waist? What about a warning shot? Why isn't that an option? Cops go through all this training to prepare for their jobs, but why isn't shooting below the waist part of the training? If it is part of the training, why is this not happening? Now, it makes sense to shoot someone in their upper body if you see the suspect is holding a gun. But shooting someone multiple times or in the chest because you fear for your life is not a good excuse. Cops know what they are signing up for, and dealing with bad people is part of the job. Just like boxers or MMA fighters—you know when you decided to do those things for a living. You know that someone is going to be constantly trying to knock you out, and that is a part of the job. For cops, they know everyone is not going to respond to them gracefully. The excuse they "feel threatened" speaks to a bigger issue with society.

Feeling threatened is a term cops have started using when killing black men. Even though these are the same cops who deal with aggressive people all the time, only a black man makes them feel threatened? If it was not just black men, why are there not as many innocent people of other races dying? Why are there constantly black men getting shot and killed, or even worse, detained, and then killed? All over, there are black people who are becoming more angry, disgusted, and confused as to why black men are constantly seen as being a threat and being killed because of that perceived threat. The shock is gone, and when you take shock out of a situation, people become more enraged and start questioning the intentions of the person or group of people who is causing these feelings. Unfortunately, these bad cops or cops who make the wrong decisions impact how black people view the police. Even worse, they create more conflict with the people they are "Protecting and Serving."

Asset Forfeit

One of the most unfair parts of policing, and something that could have a tremendous impact, is the benefits that cops/police departments get when they bust a suspect for drug crimes. If a suspect has assets, the cops can take them. Asset forfeiture is a law that allows law enforcement to take assets that might have been used to commit a crime. The catch is, even if the crime was not committed by the owner of the property, the assets can still be seized. The biggest example of this that happens routinely is the case of drug dealers. When a cop arrests a drug dealer, during that process if they find money, cars, or really anything that can produce value, they are entitled to these items. We have all heard of police auctions. The things they auction off come from these drugs dealers or people who have a lot of assets. The issue with this is that when you give a police department awards for busting drug deals, they have more of an incentive to be corrupt and skew the story of what actually happened. We can all act like every cop who does a job is honest and has high integrity, but we all know that is not the case. There are bad apples working in all industries, and when tempted with instant gratification, everyone responds differently.

The million-dollar question is, how can we have cops do their jobs and not benefit from the assets they seize? Simple. What about putting it back into the city where they get the money from such as, school systems, health care, and federal funding? The list can go on and on. It is extremely odd that the people who make the arrests and write the reports for the suspects are the same people who benefit from these people getting in trouble. This would be like if you were able to give your coworker a rating and determine their bonus for the year, and whatever money was left, you get that portion. How fair would you actually be to your co-worker if you knew you would get all the benefits from them having a lower rating? These criminals are playing a big role in funding their precincts!

Conclusion

Our system is something that works for people who have money, people who are not engulfed in the system, people who work for the system, and people who profit from the system. By no means do suspects need to have the upper hand when they are being looked at for a crime. If we are truly a country where we say someone is innocent until proven guilty, why don't suspects get any leniency during the process? Unless you have money and can pay your way out of sitting in jail, or you can pay to get yourself a great attorney, many people become a number in the system. How is this helpful? Unfortunately, or fortunately—depending on who you ask, black people are victims of a system that seems like it was meant to keep people who are less fortunate down. The money that is being made from fictional crimes or made up situations is sad, and what is even worse is that these people do not have the means to get themselves out of this situation. They end up being funneled through the system and branded a criminal. It is important to remember that discipline should be *for* someone and not *to* someone.

Just think, some people go to prison for 15 years for having drugs on them, and when they are released from jail, they are labeled a felon. What options are available to these people? Who is there to make sure they have all the tools necessary to bounce back and become functioning members of society? This is the fallout from having a system that jails you for nonviolent crimes for extended periods of time, then releases you with labels that work against you. We claim to be one of the most advanced countries in the world and the most powerful, yet we take power away from our own people because they do not have the money to get themselves out of trouble. We have all made bad decisions in life, but the difference between some of us who do not have felonies on our record and the ones that do, is we either did not get caught, we caught a break, or we were too young for it to impact our lives as adults.

Where justice is denied, where poverty is enforced, where ignorance prevails, and where any one class is made to feel that society is an organized conspiracy to oppress, rob and degrade them, neither persons nor property will be safe.

~ Frederick Douglass

Nine

NEGLECTED AMERICA

...indivisible

J im Crow was a law that allowed for racial segregation. It was not revoked until 1965. Segregation is defined as a group of people being separated in public, including anything that is public property such as schools, transportation, as well as restrooms and restaurants. Similarly, during this time, blacks were inferior to whites on basis of economic, educational, and social levels. Blacks also dealt with housing segregation, unfair bank lending practices, job discrimination, and other things that placed limits on blacks being able to give themselves a better life. Each of these things is mentioned because looking at how black people are treated now and the limitations they continue to encounter, shows that a lot of these things are still happening. If we want to act like black people are treated with the same privileges that white people are, we are only delaying the process of actually making things fair.

Acknowledging that we are a country that still treats black people unequally does not mean we are failing. It means we still have room for improvement. Some of the things that will be discussed in this section may alert some people who are unaware of what continues to happen on a daily basis. Understand that just because you are not aware of these things does not mean that they do not happen. This section is extremely important to appreciate the struggles that black people endure every single day, and hopefully, it will provide some context for people who are not familiar with these struggles.

Black Communities

One of the things America does well for other countries is to render aid and support during natural disasters. If there is an earthquake, tsunami, fire, landslide, or any other kind of natural disaster in another country, the chances of the USA sending aid or helping raise money for the situation is very high. Not only do we offer aid through our military, but our first responders and even celebrities are willing to extend a hand to help. In addition, news coverage generates attention to these issues as well. My questions are, where was the news coverage for the first year and a half of the Flint Crisis? What about the news coverage on what was going on in the inner cities like Chicago, Memphis, Detroit, Baltimore, and Oakland, just to name a few? The answer is simple; these communities are predominately black communities, and for some reason, society does not accept these situations as issues that need attention.

In Flint, Michigan, there was lead in the water system. As a result, houses had to be blocked off for professional treatment. This harmful substance was in the water, water that children were drinking, people were washing their clothes in, preparing food with, and bathing in. The worst part of the water contamination is that politicians knew what was happening, and they did nothing about it. It was not until the news came along and started putting a spotlight on Flint that people started to pay attention and take action. If you are naïve enough to think the water crisis was a surprise, how and why did General Motors use a special connection to clean their water? Their parts were rusting from the contamination and they were given another option. But what about the people and children in Flint, Michigan? On the surface, the only thing the media has made us aware of was the lead in the water. But the truth is that there could have been all kinds of diseases in that water. The water was brown! Imagine brushing your teeth with that water.

How would you feel? How could city and government officials let this happen? Do you think you would see this happen in Beverly Hills or Buckhead? Of course not, because in this country if you have money you are essentially safe from having to worry about whether your life is worth the city or state doing everything they can to keep you safe.

Consider other low-income, predominately black neighborhoods. Just like the people in Flint, Michigan, they are left to fend for themselves. Police departments think by placing a cop car in these neighborhoods they are doing a great job and preventing crimes. But when you actually look at these neighborhoods, they are riddled with crimes, killings, and are unsafe environments. The schools children attend are dirty and poorly maintained, yet we expect these children to grow up and think people have their best interests at heart. Earlier in this book, I presented a challenge for people to drive through low-income areas and look around. How would you grow up if every day you had to see pain, struggle, loss, and instability? What is America doing to help these cities? Where is their bailout? Where are the fundraisers? The news coverage? Where are supplies to help them get back on their feet? Instead, these are the people who are victimized and profiled by police, blamed for crimes they did not commit, and abandoned to fend for themselves. When is the last time you saw someone released from prison after 10+ years, for a crime they did not commit, who was rich? This only happens to poor, black people. Unfortunately, in these neighborhoods, children learn more about defending themselves and defending their "territories" than they learn about setting goals and planning for their futures. But what does our society do to help? We write them off and allow all of this chaos to happen. That way when it does, we can move in and take over their neighborhoods.

Hurricane Katrina happened in New Orleans, Louisiana, in August of 2005. This was a tremendous hurricane that was responsible for displacing millions of local communities, including many low-income black people who lived there. The sad part about this disaster is it could have been prevented. It was not a secret that the levees were not strong enough to hold if a storm of Katrina's magnitude were to happen. But instead of the city or state acknowledging the problem, instead of fixing the problem, they did nothing, and Hurricane Katrina happened. This was a catastrophe! On the news, there were stories of looting, people standing on top of cars, houses, or anything they could use to save their lives and hopefully be rescued. Why was nothing done to prevent this from happening? Why wasn't it a priority?

The only consistent conclusion to be drawn from these three examples is that when it comes to lower-income areas and areas that are predominantly black, we should not expect our country will have compassion for the way they live and the consequences that befall them. What is worse is that there is a lack of resources. There is no school for children that we should allow to be un-organized, ill equipped, under-staffed, or poorly maintained! We want people to be educated, but we permit schools in these neighborhoods to look like prisons. What message does that send? Where is the money to help these neighborhoods recover? It is so easy to talk about what a group of people should do and ways they should improve their lives, but what if, throughout your entire life, all you had experienced convinced you that you do not matter? How do you recover from that? It is like being in an abusive relationship, and when you start feeling good about yourself or when you start thinking, you can find a way out. You can look around at your environment and it seems overwhelming. Look at these situations for what they are. Black people live in a country that prides itself on helping other nations, but has millions of people living in poverty in their own country.

Gentrification
The places mentioned above and cities like Austin, Houston, New York, Atlanta, Seattle, Oregon, and Minneapolis, just to name a few, have experienced gentrification over the past 10-15 years. Gentrification means to renovate or improve. The neighborhoods are buying house or raising taxes and building and renovating houses, condos, and other amenities. By keeping the prices high, it drives people who cannot afford

these higher prices out of their homes. In layman's terms, black people are being displaced out of their neighborhoods because their taxes are going up, and they can no longer afford their places of residence. Blacks move out and wealthier people build.

Why does this happen? Well we can say the cities are growing rapidly, and with more people moving into these desirable cities, it causes prices to go up. However, what really happens is places black people used to call home are now becoming expensive desirable areas, and these poorer black families now have to make a life somewhere else. So, it is no longer enough that for decades the city/state refused to invest money or attention in these neighborhoods, now, when they do decide to put money back into them, existing residents have to leave the area and will not be a part of the rebuilding. If you raise taxes in areas where people live and they can no longer afford to live there, they have to move or sell. Then what happens is whoever buys the property comes in and renovates. In addition, the house value shoots up sometimes 50% or more in price. That means that someone in a different tax bracket will move into to that house. Since this person in a higher tax bracket does not want to live next to people in a lower tax bracket, over time the neighborhood becomes gentrified as wealthier people drive out poorer people. What used to be a low-income area becomes a middle to upper class neighborhood. Sounds great, right? Sure, unless you are the black people who are being displaced by all of this.

I am from Austin, Texas and I have watched this transition happen. There used to be a sizeable population of blacks who lived on the East side of Austin, close to downtown. However, as Austin has become more desirable, East Austin is no longer what it used to be. Million dollar condos are now there, houses are being flipped and sold at a higher value, and East Austin is completely different from what it once was. The area has changed drastically. I If you are rich, you have a desirable place to live. If you cannot afford it, you have to relocate and start your life somewhere else. This is sad, but as mentioned before, this is a way to get black people out of the way to create a more affluent neighborhood. Look at New Orleans now and the houses that were built in the places where the low-income areas once were. The people who lived there before could not go back and live in New Orleans if they wanted to. They experienced a disaster, but people who can afford more expensive homes benefited from Katrina. Just in case you are wondering, yes, they fixed the levees. There was a reason to. They had to protect the more affluent people who moved in to replace the lower-income people who had to vacate. Think about this for a second. Use your common sense and ask yourself why this is happening? Once again, ask yourself who benefits from this situation and who loses?

Racial Profiling

Unfortunately, every single day black people are racially profiled and harassed, no matter where they are, who they are, or what they are doing. Recently, in the news, James Blake provides an example of how blacks are treated on a daily basis. James Blake was tackled and detained on a suspicion of committing a crime, even though he provided identification. Videos that have been recorded or viewed by people all over the world, show cops harassing black people in their cars, walking down the street, or anywhere else. The simple fact that cops can use the idea that they "feel threatened" as an excuse to kill black people is an example of racial profiling because what they are really saying is since the person is black they felt threatened. How many times have you gone to an event and seen a white person yelling at a cop or engaging in behaviors that are completely disrespectful? They are not met with deadly force. Half the time, they are not even arrested. The cops just ask them to stop behaving the way they are. These cops have guns, and in most cases, back-up from other officers. But they are the ones that feel threatened, just because someone is black? How does that make sense?

There are certain patterns of racial profiling that happen repeatedly to black people. Being followed in department stores, police officers questioning you for no reason, being stereotyped, driving while black, living in a white-dominated neighborhood, servers treating your table differently from other tables, the list goes on. This happens constantly no matter where black people are. What makes this even worse is how black men get treated. They are usually the ones who are profiled, more than women, because they are seen as intimidating and strong. This is where "feeling threatened" comes into play. Black men in America face struggles that most people do not realize or understand. The idea that they are a threat just by their appearance is a start, but even the way they dress, the type of job they have, how their hair is done, and their tone of voice are just a few things that can be strikes against these men. No matter what a black man does, they will be crucified because they are expected to be perfect and unbreakable. But society forgets they are also humans!

Fatherless Homes

Another big problem that black people experience is growing up in fatherless homes. Yes, some of these fatherless homes happen because the men decided to leave their homes. However, when you take a look at jails and prisons and see who is getting arrested more, it is black people, and in particular, black men. This creates a trickle-down effect on the homes these black men come from and impacts their children. This dismantling of black families creates so many difficult circumstances, and can be the start of patterns repeating themselves. For example, if a black man gets pulled over by a police officer on a suspension of a crime, more times than not, the black person will be ticketed or arrested. Either way, the person either goes to jail or receives a ticket. In either instance money has to be paid to get out of trouble. If the worst happens and they go to jail, the cycle of being in the quicksand starts and the person has to pay their way out of jail. If they cannot afford that, then it is a rapid, and unforgiving ripple-down effect that starts with them staying in jail, and progresses through losing their job, and costing their family more money—all because of a suspicion. Think about the impact this has on a family.

It feels as though removing black men from homes can be a win for the prison systems because they can make money from having this person locked up. A man has been removed from his home causing negative downfalls for his family, and the worst part of this is that it impacts the children. Yes, black men have responsibilities in some of their arrests, and yes, sometimes they are guilty. But sometimes is not a good enough reason to put someone behind bars and cause a family pain and suffering. Having a fatherless home can start a cycle for children to follow in their father's footsteps. Think about how many single parent homes this creates, or how this could impact the amount of supervision from parents a child loses.

Conclusion

Jim Crow is still very much alive, and black people are still treated as less than. Has it gotten better? Well, in some aspects. Is there still a level of inferiority and segregation that happens? Of course. Look at these examples. This information is not made up, nor did it come from one person or one family. this is reality for a lot of people. This is what they wake up to, deal with during the daytime, and fall asleep dealing with. This is their life in a country where we are told everyone is treated fairly and everyone has the same opportunities. Understand the anger and aggressiveness that you see on the news starts in neighborhoods where people constantly experience injustices. Why do you think the protests bring out so many people of all races?

There is unfair treatment happening all over black communities, as well as to black people who are in society. Black people are tired of feeling like we do not matter. People are more willing to help a dog fight for their rights than they are willing to help black people who are human beings. How do we help blacks? Every time an artist tries to make music or a celebrity comes out with facts about the struggle of black people, they are condemned and people try to discredit what they have to say. Why does this happen? Why can't black people be uplifted? What is the harm in that?

Even mass murders a re treated better than black people. Robert Lewis Dear, Dylann Roof, James Holmes, Jason Dalton, and Jared Loughner were all white men who were responsible for mass murders. Each of them is still alive and telling their story. Each story involves guns, violence, and trying to avoid cops. But none of them was shot, or worse, killed by cops. On the other hand, you have black men who are *suspects* in crimes, but when cops see them, they "feel threatened." Does that give them the right to draw guns and shoot to kill?

The problem of the twentieth century is the problem of the color line.

~ W. E. B. Du Bois

Ten

WHAT CAN WE DO BETTER

...with liberty and

Part of being black is being aware of the inequities you could face at any moment. Being aware of this does not mean that you have to accept that nothing can change, or that it cannot get better. Just because society has placed judgements and stereotypes on us, does not mean that is who we are. Through all of our ups and downs, we can have a positive impact on the turnaround of how black people are treated. Thus far in this book, the topics have been about the ways in which black people are excluded and treated as second class citizens. However, we do not have to play the role of victim. In fact, there are a lot of ways that we can control how society views and treats us.

We must know our history and not let it repeat itself. Slavery is a part of our history, and being treated as less than a human, is part of our past. In order to have a better future, we must accept these facts and find better ways to progress. Solutions to problems do not happen overnight, and we owe it to ourselves, families, friends, and the future of this country to make sure our own behavior is in line with how we want to be perceived. Every single person in this country has the capability to make these inequities disappear, and for us, there are ways for all to become unified.

Support

If we are going to make this shift as a country, we have to start with ourselves! If we do not believe, support, respect, and cherish each other, how can we expect others to? No longer is it justifiable to not support black businesses or kill each other. We are all fighting the same fight, and yes, some of us have it better than others. Some of us might not understand each other, but that is not an excuse to wage a war against one another; we are all we have. It is important for black people and black communities to come together. What is the difference between a black community and black people? A black community is a place that has black people living in close quarters. Black people are people who are black—who might not live in the black communities, but still go through the same inequities that black communities experience. Black people who come from neighborhoods of struggle do not always get respect from black people who do not understand their struggles and vice versa. This is a division that has to stop—if we divide ourselves within our own race, we are no better than the society that divides us.

We might not understand each other, but it is our job to try. We should support the positives that people are trying to achieve. At the very least, we need to understand each other's struggles. Some of us are fortunate enough to have a platform or an audience. Take for instance this book; it is my hope that on some levels this can be a tool to open people's eyes about life and about being black. This is not just meant for white people, but all people including other blacks! I am using this as a platform to garner attention for something that is out of control, and is detrimental to our race. Having people read about the struggles we face will hopefully create some conversations and movement toward blacks being treated fairly. Sometimes people who are seen as criminals are just people trapped in a system that has more to gain by labeling them as criminals, than giving them a fair chance to prosper. If we all make the decision today that we are going to support each other and respect each other, things will change because we are a stronger force together. It is important to believe that together we have more power than we think.

We Need to Participate

We have to be active participants in society. What does this mean? Voting is a big part, and giving you opportunities to make better decisions are ways to be more active. Voting is a right that our ancestors lost their lives for. Not only that, but how can we expect to see change if we do not participate in events that can change laws? It is no longer good enough to just talk about things that should change. We have to participate in creating that change. No law is enacted without support (votes). While everyone talks about the importance of voting for the president, it is just as important, if not more important, to make sure we vote in city council elections too. This is where the laws start to enter into the conversation, and if we are active earlier in these processes, imagine how much we could impact.

How many black people reading this book have good credit? How many of you can walk into a car dealership, and you know with certainty that you will be able to get an APR that you want? If you are not in that place, somewhere along the line wrong decisions were made. Making the wrong decisions is a part of life, but fixing those bad decisions is where our energy needs to be spent. It is important, as black people, to stop this trend. We need to start making better decisions so we can have better credit. Good credit can be the difference between living in an apartment versus buying a house, and getting a new car versus having to buy a cash car. There are so many other advantages, and we have to educate ourselves to be in a position where our credit scores start to be a part of bettering our lives.

Lastly, it is important that we provide secure, respectful, and realistic role models for our black children. It is important that our children do not grow up with role models who cannot speak to the hard times black people have dealt with. Allowing celebrities to be our children's role models sets them up to idolize people who do not even see themselves as role models. These men and women who impact our children's lives cannot know what our children are going through because they are not there on a daily basis.

Real role models, ones who will have the most lasting impact on a child, are people they can relate to and whom they see often. This gives them someone to talk to when they struggle and the opportunity to watch their role model overcome life's obstacles. It is important that even as adults we have role models who provide us a safe place. Just as children need guidance, adults need mentors, role models, and trusted supporters. Being able to bounce your ideas or decisions off someone whom you trust and respect can make a world of difference as you go through life. It is our job to provide children with positive and motivated role models. Ask yourselves:

1. Are you a role model?
2. Do you have a role model?
3. Who can I help by being their role model?

Each of the answers to these questions can make all the difference in the world for everyone involved. Parents, siblings, cousins, classmates, teammates, and teachers are all people who should be role models. These people should know you well and be able to respect your goals and give you guidance if need be.

Social Media

Social media is one of the best and worst things that has happened to black people. On the one hand when injustice happens to black people via police brutality or even discriminatory conversations, they can be recorded. We also now have a place where we can talk about how we feel, share memes that we can identify with, and engage in ways that five years ago, we were not able to. Protests have been organized thanks to social media, and people have been able to get stories out that might not otherwise have gotten out. Even though all of these things are great, I cannot help but think about the adverse effects that social media has had on black people. Between Twitter, Facebook, and Instagram some black people find themselves competing and comparing their lives to others. Some people go to these social media outlets to determine what stage of life they should be in, or even worse, getting advice from people who know nothing about your real life.

Of course these social media outlets are not just hampering black people; they are having a negative effect on how we communicate with each other. It is important to remember that social media is not the end all be all. People still have to communicate and get to know each other on a level that goes far beyond user names. As black people, we are all going through something. We all have moments of being fragile and having things that are not pleasant happen to us. We are avoiding being vulnerable. We must not use social media as a place to act like our lives are better than they are. Be honest with yourself and what you stand for. Do not get sucked into the fiction of social media because you will become just as fictitious as the posts you are posting. For those of you who do not like this section or feel offended, maybe you are someone who needs to reevaluate your relationship with social media.

Pissing on your Own Leg

When we get opportunities we cannot afford to mess them up. It is not often that a black person catches a break, so when we do, it is important to make the best of the opportunity. An example of this break is when someone gets a full scholarship to play a sport in college, and they jeopardize it by getting into trouble. The same can be said for professional athletes! When you get to a place that most people only dream of, make the best of that situation. When you get that dream job, do not lose it because of dumb decisions. If you get accepted into a university, fill out your paperwork and meet the deadlines. Do not waste it, jeopardize it, trivialize it, or lose it by making a poor decision.

In this year's Super Bowl, Cam Newton had a golden opportunity to show his growth as a person and athlete. All season he danced around when his team won and drew comparisons to some of the best quarterbacks to ever play in the NFL. During the game, things did not go well, and instead of coming out and talking after the game at a press conference, he decided to not say anything during the interview. We can act like he was hearing other interviews and we can make all the excuses in the world for him. However, Tom Brady and Peyton Manning have both lost in Super Bowls, and they came out and did interviews and answered the tough questions. So if we want to be in a situation where we are compared to the best and want to make the most of our circumstances, we cannot shy away from things that are not going our way. We have to take accountability for our actions, whether we get a desired outcome or not.

The same can be said for hit televisions shows and musicians. When you catch a break and you are on a great show or when you are involved in big collaborations—do not mess that up! This does not happen to everyone, so when it does happen, we have to seize the opportunity. As black people, if we want businesses, people, entertainment, and opportunities for our country to see how great black people are, we cannot ruin opportunities by making poor decisions. Remember, you are setting that path for the next black person to know they can have high standards for their lives. It is up to each of us to be a part of the foundation for the path to success.

Doubting someone else's Blackness

Lastly, but most importantly, we have to stop doubting or knocking anyone's blackness! Just because someone speaks properly or is educated does not make them more or less of a black person than another black person. There is no such thing as a "real black person," or "not black," or an "oreo." Society already tells us what they consider "black," and apparently, society says if you speak like an uneducated individual and you live in a low-income neighborhood, that justifies you as a real black person. But what does that say about us if we believe these ridiculous labels? Being black is not a bad thing, and we should not come with labels. We are not *less than* as a group, and we need to remember that we can be just as educated, inventive, supportive, and brilliant as any other race.

Every black person has their own black experience. Moments where you know your skin color was the reason you were treated differently is a part of this experience. So we do not need to discredit each other, no matter how privileged you might think someone is. Our skin color is still black. Look at President Obama and consider how he is treated— and, he has the most prestigious job in America.

Conclusion

We are taught to hate and fight each other. I instead, let's learn to respect and guide each other through life. We support famous people we do not even know, but we will not support people we have known for years. Why? It is pretty obvious now that the "War on Drugs" was essentially a war on black people because drugs have gotten worse since the "war" was declared. Let's make the choice today to be more influential. We have a chance to be a part of the solution and accept who we are. We can positively influence our situations, and we have to make that decision. Everyone will have a different solution to the problem and that is fine. The important thing is that we fix it and be resilient through all this pain and disappointment. We must all do our part in changing the perceptions people have about us. At this point, we are all aware that cops benefit more by black people being in jail and being in trouble because we become a source of income. So possessing this knowledge should allow us to make better decisions! Let's not be *victims* of circumstances; let's *create* better circumstances.

"A race of people is like an individual man; until it uses its own talent, takes pride in its own history, expresses its own culture, affirms its own selfhood, it can never fulfill itself."

~ Malcolm X

Eleven

THE POWER OF INTENTION

...justice for all

Final Thoughts

Take a look at the things in this world that continuously tell black people they are not good enough. Look at the schools our children are in and the low-income neighborhoods; what is out there that shows black people how much they matter? Pay attention to which people are locked up in jails and how long their sentences are versus others. Consider how black people cringe when a cop pulls up behind them. What do people have to worry about when they are isolated in schools or at work? Look at our entertainment business. Whose faces do you constantly see? Who gets credit for bringing attention to black culture?

If you have gotten to this point in the book, and you feel like I am way off topic and I have over exaggerated the things that happen to black people, do your own research online or ask a black person. If that still fails to convince you these things are happening, I feel sorry for you. You live in a world where you will not allow yourself to be open to the realities that others are going through. Black people are not the enemy. This country is supposed to be *of* the *people*, *by* the *people*, and *for* the *people*; this includes black people.

How Can WE Fix This

Collectively, we have to come together and fix the things that are broken. We must come together and support one another no matter your race or background. Remember, with support comes educating each other. It is imperative that we see each other as teammates and not as enemies or competitors. As people, we all have the power to be the change that we want to see. If you are reading this book and you like the treatment of black people and you like the inequalities that we experience, then shame on you. This could easily be you or someone that you know. It is time to be honest, talk about conflict, and most importantly, it is time that we listen, without judging other people's journeys. There is already so much hate in this world; why not spread some love and acceptance?

Being Aware

Just to be clear, other races face racism, as well. But black people have dealt with it for centuries, and it seems as though we take two steps forward and five steps back. It is no longer acceptable to blatantly be a racist, so now, people have to find indirect ways to try and limit the successes and evolutions of black people. Being black is not just a race, and it comes with labels and stereotypes that must stop. Some black people are tired of being tired, but now, we have to fight and push through. There has to be a cultural awareness for all of us so that we can understand other people's perspectives. As human beings, we all want to be accepted and we all want to be treated fairly. What reason do we have to not make that happen?

We have to be blind to race because race is not enough of a reason to treat someone unfairly. If you are someone who feels like another race is bad or if you harbor bad feelings for another race, ask yourself why this is the case. After you answer those questions, ask yourself how you are helping the community become a better place. I am not sure about you, but I would like to leave this earth better than the way I found it. I would like my children and their children to truly feel like the sky is the limit. Right now ISIS is killing and harming innocent civilians and destroying cities. Children and women are being beaten and treated unfairly. We have a major drug problem that impacts all of our communities. When you look at all of these issues we have to ask ourselves why are we wasting our time embracing racism toward black people, when black people are dealing with these same issues? We are people, and we all have heartbeats and blood running through our veins. We all have fears, and we all have aspirations. How much more pleasant would it be to put love in the air versus spreading hate and isolation?

Laying a Solid Foundation

Every single one of us is responsible for the decisions we make. We must start laying solid foundations within our families, friends, and anyone that we come into contact with. The world is changing, and we have to evolve with the changes. Racism and the exclusion of black people should no longer be acceptable. Labels have no place in our society. These labels play a role in the demise of our own citizens. So, do your own research and stop depending on the news to tell you the whole story. It is not their job to tell us the whole story; it is only their job to give us information they believe people want to hear. Information is essential to humans, and we must feed ourselves with knowledge. Step out of the comfort zones we live in and trust our abilities to see races as equal. How can we all be a piece of the country that can together become progressive? Let's plan to not be programmed and make it a priority to see people for who they are, and not what we are told about who they are. Humble yourselves; this world is ours to make better.

One Last Thought

Our U.S. Constitution Preamble reads as follows:

"We the People of the United States, in order to form a more perfect Union, establish Justice, insure domestic tranquility, provide for the common defence, promote the general welfare and secure the Blessing of Liberty to ourselves and our posterity do ordain and establish this Constitution for the United States of America."

This is supposed to be what we pride ourselves on and what we stand for as Americans. Think about your life, and ask yourself if you are choosing to treat everyone like they should be treated? Are you adhering to the things said in the U.S. Constitution? If not, it is time to start heading in a different direction.

Reflect on the 10 words that were included in the introduction:

1. Rich
2. Aggressive
3. Happiness
4. Black Man
5. Police Officer
6. Lawyer
7. Teacher
8. Athletes
9. Loud
10. Smart

Ask yourself if your opinion has changed on what comes to mind when you think of those words? We are a society that prides itself on being free and equal, and it is time that we put those thoughts into action. Just because you do not like things that have been said in this book does not mean they are not true, or that they do not happen. For black people, we must have dignity in the face of ignorance and realize that we are worthy of respect and opportunities. Every single morning you wake up you have a choice. What choices are you going to make today?

Success is to be measured not so much by the position that one has reached in life as by the obstacles which he has overcome.

~ Booker T. Washington